THE CHICAGO PUBLIC LIBRARY

FORM 19

DEC   1988

The Cinema and Ireland

Also by Anthony Slide

Early American Cinema (1970)
The Griffith Actresses (1973)
The Idols of Silence (1976)
The Big V: A History of the Vitagraph Company (1976; revised 1987)
Early Women Directors (1977; revised 1984)
Aspects of American Film History Prior to 1920 (1978)
Films on Film History (1979)
The Kindergarten of the Movies: A History of the Fine Arts Company (1980)
The Vaudevillians (1981)
Great Radio Personalities in Historic Photographs (1982)
A Collector's Guide to Movie Memorabilia (1983)
Fifty Classic British Films: 1932-1982 (1985)
A Collector's Guide to TV Memorabilia (1985)
The American Film Industry: A Historical Dictionary (1986)
The Great Pretenders (1986)
Fifty Classic French Films: 1912-1982 (1987)

With Edward Wagenknecht

The Films of D.W. Griffith (1975)
Fifty Great American Silent Films: 1912-1920 (1980)

As Editor

Selected Film Criticism: 1896-1911 (1982)
Selected Film Criticism: 1912-1920 (1982)
Selected Film Criticism: 1921-1930 (1982)
Selected Film Criticism: 1931-1940 (1982)
Selected Film Criticism: 1941-1950 (1982)
Selected Film Criticism: Foreign Films 1930-1950 (1984)
Selected Film Criticism: 1951-1960 (1985)
International Film, Radio, and Television Journals (1985)
Selected Theatre Criticism: 1900-1919 (1985)
Selected Theatre Criticism: 1920-1930 (1985)
Selected Theatre Criticism: 1931-1950 (1986)
Filmfront (1986)
Selected Radio and Television Criticism (1987)

The Cinema and Ireland

by
Anthony Slide

McFarland & Company, Inc., Publishers
Jefferson, North Carolina, and London

"The people are too lazy, and the weather is too bad for anyone to care for anything except the church and the cinema."

Micheál Mac Liammóir in *All for Hecuba*

Library of Congress Cataloguing-in-Publication Data

Slide, Anthony.
   The cinema and Ireland / by Anthony Slide.
    p.   cm.
   Bibliography: p.
   Includes index.
   ISBN 0-89950-322-5
   1. Moving-pictures—Ireland. 2. Moving-pictures, American-
-Ireland. 3. English literature—Irish authors—History and
criticism. 4. Moving-pictures and literature. 5. Ireland in motion
pictures. I. Title.
PN1993.5.I85S55 1988
791.43'09415—dc19   87-29880
                                                                                                    CIP

© 1988 Anthony Slide. All rights reserved.

Printed in the United States of America (acid-free natural paper)

McFarland & Company, Inc., Publishers
   Box 611, Jefferson, North Carolina 28640

Table of Contents

Introduction   vi

I. Native Irish Film Production   1
II. The American Film Producer in Ireland   39
III. Irish Literature and the Cinema   53
IV. The Irishman in Hollywood   73
V. The Irish Image on American Screens   99

Notes   115
Bibliography   117
Index   121

Introduction

To many, the idea of a book devoted to Irish cinema must be comparable to a volume on the snakes of Ireland. There are none of the latter and little of the former. However, Ireland has nourished a native film industry, albeit at times almost nonexistent. It has also contributed considerably to filmmaking in the United States and elsewhere through Irish talent and Irish literary efforts. Although it is only a small country, with a population of approximately three million people in the Republic of Ireland (Eire) and one million in Northern Ireland (Ulster), there is much of which the country can feel proud as regards its film heritage.

Sadly, from a cultural viewpoint, Ireland has done exceedingly little to document its heritage. Along with Albania, it is the only country in Europe without a national film archive. Between 1936 and 1976, it did boast the Irish Film Society, which presented screenings of important historical and foreign-language films throughout the country, and which also published intermittently from 1945 through 1968 a journal titled *Scannán*. The first film periodical in Ireland was *The Irish Limelight*, a trade paper published in Dublin from January 1917 through December 1920 on a monthly basis. Currently, there is only one serious film journal emanating from Ireland, and that is *Film Directions*, first published on a quarterly basis in 1977 and sponsored by the Arts Council of Northern Ireland and the Arts Council of Eire. Interestingly, *Film Directions* has published only one Irish film critic/journalist of any merit, and that is Kevin Rockett.

The educational use of the motion picture was, and continues to be, stressed by the National Film Institute of Ireland (Institiuid Naisunta na Scannain), which was established in 1943 as a Catholic organization. The Irish government (Dail Eireann) made a small, yearly grant to the Institute, which built up a fine library of 16mm films available for rental throughout the Republic. The Institute also published a quarterly journal, *Vision*, in which this writer's first articles on the history of filmmaking in Ireland appeared.

The work of preserving and documenting Irish film history has been left, almost by default, to one individual, Liam O'Leary, who had written the first book on the history of motion pictures to be published in Ireland, *Introduction to the Film*, and had been associated for many years with the British

Introduction vii

The founders of the Irish Film Society. Liam O'Leary is standing in the middle of the back row.

National Film Archive. In 1976, O'Leary organized an exhibition, "Cinema Ireland," at Trinity College, Dublin, as part of the Dublin Arts Festival. That exhibition became the impetus for his creating the Liam O'Leary Film Archives, which he operates out of his Dublin apartment, and which has become the central repository for papers and films relating to Irish cinema history. Back in April 1978, Liam O'Leary formally announced the existence of his archives, with three official "foreign correspondents": Kevin Brownlow in London, Lotte Eisner (now deceased) in Paris, and this writer in Los Angeles.

This book owes a great deal to Liam O'Leary in that he encouraged my earliest writing on film history in England in the late sixties, and also offered me hospitality on a number of visits to Dublin in the sixties and seventies. I do not always agree with Liam's findings and opinions, and I suspect this present volume will not meet with his total approval.

The first draft of this book was prepared more than 16 years ago. At that time, my acknowledgments page noted more than six years spent in researching the topic. Since that time I have added to my researches, and it is perhaps not incorrect to state that *The Cinema and Ireland* is the result of more than 20 years of study on the subject. In that I am an Englishman, rather than an Irishman, I suspect that I will draw a considerable amount of critical fire, in much the same way as my having the audacity to be a man and write a book on early women directors back in 1977 drew criticism from feminists. My response to such criticism is simply that someone should write a book on these subjects, and if I am the only individual willing to devote the time to such projects, so be it.

Research for this book was undertaken in three countries: in Ireland, at the National Library of Ireland; in the United Kingdom, at the British Film Institute; and in the United States, at the Margaret Herrick Library of the Academy of Motion Picture Arts and Sciences, the Library of Congress, and the Doheny Memorial Library of the University of Southern California.

Several people, now deceased, were helpful: Eileen Crowe, Micheál Mac Liamóir, and Hilton Edwards. In Dublin, I would like to thank Alf Mac Lochlainn, George Morrison, and, of course, Liam O'Leary. Seldom a day goes by that I do not remember with affection Audrey Melbourne-Cooper, a dear friend in London, who talked with me often about the work of her father, Arthur Melbourne-Cooper. Vernon Whitten corresponded with me from South Africa regarding the Irish career of his father, Norman. In Killarney, Miss Annie O'Sullivan and I spent a very pleasant afternoon discussing the visits of Sidney Olcott and the Kalem Company to Beaufort. My interest in this project was rekindled in a large part by Bob Brien, who invited me to be Hollywood adviser for his five-part 1984 Ulster Television series, *A Seat Among the Stars: The Cinema and Ireland*.

My thoughts on John Ford are, in part, based on conversations with two members of his stock company, the late Frank Baker and Ruth Clifford. I am also grateful for Mary Ford's spending the time to discuss her husband's life and career.

Fielder Cook spoke with me at length on the making of the first feature film at Ardmore Studios, *Home Is the Hero*, which he directed.

In *The Irish Statesman* for June 9, 1928, W.B. Yeats wrote of the motion picture that "the whole history of the world must be reduced to wallpaper in front of which the characters must pose and speak." Let this book be the "wallpaper" upon which a splendid company of Irish characters pose and speak.

Anthony Slide

I. Native Irish Film Production

The first film program to be presented before a paying audience was given by the Lumière Brothers on December 28, 1895, at the Grand Café on the Boulevard des Capucines in Paris. The first public performance in England took place at the Regent Street Polytechnic, London, on February 20, 1896. In Ireland, Dan Lowrey offered the public its first opportunity to view moving pictures at his Star of Erin Music Hall (now the Olympia Theatre) in Dublin on April 20, 1896. The presentation was not particularly successful, but Lowrey gave a second film presentation at the Star of Erin and at the Empire Variety Theatre, Belfast, in October of the same year. Other early, specialized film screenings followed; in 1897, Robert W. Paul demonstrated his "Animatographe" at the Grand Opera House, Belfast, and the Opera House, Cork; Lowrey opened the Palace Variety Theatre, Cork, in 1897 with Professor Jolly's "Cinématographe"; and the Edison films were first seen in Ireland at the Rotunda, Dublin, in November 1901.

As in most European countries, it was left to the travelling showmen to popularize the new invention and to bring the motion picture before the gaze of the rest of Ireland, where the first such film exhibitor was Professor Le Clair. In 1897, Le Clair presented the cinematograph as part of an entertainment which also included performing dogs and a well-known, Dublin-based female impersonator, Geoffrey Harrison. That same year, three more travelling showmen—James Lloyd (of Lloyd's Circus), Dr. Ormonde and Vincent Paul—also realized the potential of the motion picture as a form of entertainment.

The first films to be produced in Ireland, as elsewhere, were actualities and newsreels; one of the earliest of the latter being of the 1900 visit of Queen Victoria to Dublin. The first known Irish-born filmmaker was Thomas Horgan, a Youghal photographer, who, with his brothers James and Philip, filmed the visit of King Edward VII to Lismore Castle on May 2, 1904. According to the *Youghal Tribune* "When the brothers attempted to set up the camera outside the castle entrance they were immediately surrounded by members of the R.I.C. [Royal Irish Constabulary] and plain-clothes detectives who questioned them at length. Anarchists were very active at the time and the police who had never seen a motion picture camera feared that the strange apparatus might

1

be an infernal machine. One herculean constable insisted on standing immediately in front of the lens and it was only possible to get the picture by pushing him aside as the Royal party passed. His helmet slipped over his face and the pictures were taken before he could adjust it. However as the Queen passed in her carriage she apparently recognised the camera as such and bowing graciously she smiled into the lens." The Horgans also claimed to have pioneered the publication of picture postcards in Ireland, and they also built one of the oldest surviving cinemas in the Republic; Horgan's Picture Palace, Youghal, opened in the town's main street on St. Stephen's Night, 1917.

The cinema building was converted from a photographic studio and the Horgans' family home. Indeed, for some time half of the projection room was used as a kitchen, while the other half served as a living room. As the cinema used—and still did as recently as 1970—back projection, there was a small stage between the projection box and the screen; this place served as a bedroom!

Horgan painted pictorial representations of scenes from films on the walls of the auditorium, and although these have now disappeared, examples of Mr. Horgan's artistic endeavors are still to be seen in the foyer, the walls of which are covered by murals of country scenes. Interestingly, as recently as 1970, the auditorium still contained one row of the original wooden benches, installed when the cinema first opened.

Next to Horgan's Picture Palace stood Hurst's Picture Palace. This was burnt to the ground in 1935, when the Hurst family built the Regal Cinema opposite, which they still own and run. As might be expected, there was much rivalry between the two families. When Horgan installed sound apparatus and introduced the talkies to Youghal via M-G-M's *The Trial of Mary Dugan* (directed by Bayard Veiller and starring Norma Shearer), he advertised his films as "All Talking Pictures." Hurst, still screening silents, countered with an advertisement proclaiming, "Silent, but Sound." Thomas Horgan died on Monday, September 27, 1948.

The honor of having produced the first fictional film in Ireland must go to the English pioneer, Arthur Melbourne-Cooper, the founder of a small film-producing company known as the Alpha Trading Company, with studios at St. Albans, Hertfordshire. Born in 1874, the son of a professional photographer, Melbourne-Cooper had been responsible for one of the earliest advertising films, produced for Birds' Custard in 1897, and several puppet films, including *Dreams of Toyland* (1907) and *Noah's Ark* (1908). He died on November 24, 1961.

On September 16, 1907, the Great Western Railway Company ran the first train excursion from Paddington to Killarney. The train, pulled by engine No. 3408, covered the distance from Paddington to Fishguard in four hours, fifty-eight minutes, and the all-inclusive fare was 17*s*.6*d*. or 27*s*.6*d*., including drives, boating and two meals at the New Hotel, Killarney. Arthur Melbourne-Cooper had approached the railway company with a view to filming these excursions. The company was favorably disposed towards the idea, and Sir James Inglis, general manager and consulting engineer, arranged for a specially constructed platform to be built on the front of one of the engines, on which Melbourne-Cooper's camera was mounted. And so, on October 12, 1907, Arthur Melbourne-Cooper set out with his brother, a camera and 3,000 feet of film, eager to commence work on his epic.

Three thousand feet of film (with an average running time of 35 minutes) was a tremendous length for a film in those days. It was very unusual indeed for a production to be longer than one reel or 1,000 feet prior to 1910. When Melbourne-Cooper had first approached the Eastman Kodak Company to try to obtain the necessary film, his request was turned down. The then head of the company, Ernest Blake, refused to believe that an audience would sit through a film of such a length, and eventually Melbourne-Cooper found that the only way in which he could acquire such a large quantity of raw film stock was to become the British agent for the German Agfa Company.

From his first night in Ireland at Kelly's Hotel, Rosslare, Arthur Melbourne-Cooper found everything to his satisfaction. On September 21, he wrote back to his fiancée in England, Kate Lacey, that the filming was completed.

Entitled *London to Killarney*, the film had its premiere at Melbourne-Cooper's own cinema, the Alpha Picture Palace, St. Albans, on December 19, 1907. It was subsequently distributed in three parts by the Charles Urban Company.

Part One, titled *Glimpses of Erin*, was described as "scenes that are brightest." It showed the Giant's Causeway, Achill Island, the Gap of Dunloe, Kate Kearney's Cottage, Torc Falls, Ross Castle and Killarney by night, the last being described as "majestic and sublime."

The second part was called *Irish Life and Character*. It featured nine different scenes, beginning with boys leaving an Irish day school, followed by a flock of geese and the female pupils. The *Urban Catalogue* had this to say in its entry: "The surprised expression of the children has been happily caught as they see the Kinematograph camera for the first time in their lives. Though most of the children are barefooted and tattered, the clean, bright and intelligent faces make a beautiful picture which will arouse enthusiasm wherever shown. A delightful study of sweet Irish childhood." This scene was followed by hotel servants and guests at an alfresco dance; spinning and carding flax; an Irish jig, danced by the two oldest inhabitants of Divagh; and shooting the rapids at Killarney. Also in the *Urban Catalogue*: "a crazy picture of the same subject, taken at one-tenth the usual rate. Novel, puzzling and comical effects; perfectly natural, but apparently impossible performances."

The third part was concerned with *The Railway Run from Waterford to Wexford*, with this comment from *Catalogue*: "This subject depicts the lovely little railway run from Cork Harbour to Crosshaven. Leaving Glenbrook the train runs along the banks of the Lee to Monkstown, thence along the shores to Monkstown Bay. Charming views of river scenery are obtained, which are crowned by that of Drake's Pool, as the train sweeps round the curve about half a mile from Crosshaven." The final part showed *Transferring Mails at Queenstown* to the White Star S.S. *Baltic*.

Most important of all, however, the Charles Urban Company extracted from Melbourne-Cooper's 3,000 feet of film two short comedies, titled *Irish Wives and English Husbands* and *Belles of Killarney*. The leading parts in these knockabout slapstick comedies were taken by a local Killarney girl, Kate O'Connor, and her sister, whom Melbourne-Cooper described as "strapping great Irish girls." Miss O'Connor is said to have later gained fame—albeit anonymously—as the girl on the posters of the Great Western Railway Company, advertising its Irish excursions. As is all too often the case in the history of the Irish cinema, none of these films are now known to exist.

The only other early fictional production to be shot in Ireland appears to be the 1908 *A Cattle Drive in County Galway*, produced and directed by another British film pioneer, R.W. Paul. The British film trade journal, *The Bioscope*, gives the following detailed account of the film:

> This lawless and exciting practice is adopted by tenant farmers in order to compel an obstinate land-owner to sell his pastures to them in place of renting them to a grazier. The tenants, banded together in a league, decide on concerted action, and, on a pre-arranged signal, collect together, and drive off the grazier's cattle to some remote spot. Usually, as in the case depicted, the occasion is taken advantage of for a general demonstration, in which the local drum and fife bands, as well as the women, dressed in their best, join. On a recent occasion thirty-one men were arraigned at Galway assizes for this offence, and they very kindly arranged to repeat the scene for the purpose of this picture; over two hundred people, collected from within a radius of twenty miles, joined with their bands and banners, and about one hundred head of cattle and sheep were driven. The scenes include the calling out of the leaguers with their hazels, removing the grazier's cattle from the fields, and an attempt by the owner to restore them with the aid of the police, who are called out from the barracks, on their cycles, by a hasty messenger. There is no straining after effect in this film, which gives a true insight into one of the most extraordinary forms of popular coercion in modern Ireland.

Other filmmaking in the country at this time included newsreel coverage of the 1909 Trooping of the Colours ceremony at Dublin Castle; given its initial screening at the Round House Rotunda, Dublin. In the same year, a Mr. A.B. Malden was entertaining Irish exiles in England with a cinematograph lecture on *Picturesque Ireland*, which opened in Westminster Cathedral Hall, London, on St. Patrick's Eve. The cinema seems to have been a favorite means of helping Irishmen abroad feel a little nearer home. In 1912, a cinematograph and concert party, calling themselves "Ireland Today," toured Australia with 150 items of film in color to screen while they sang Irish songs and ballads.

On April 9, 1910, the Sackville Picture House, situated at 51 Lower

Sackville Street, Dublin, was opened by Sir Charles Cameron. The theatre was owned by the London-based Provincial Cinematograph Theatres, and according to a report in *The Film Index* (October 15, 1910), "It was the first of its kind to open in Ireland and from its inception has been an unqualified success. The theatre opens daily at 2 o'clock, and a continuous performance is given until 10:30. The theatre is furnished and equipped in the most up-to-date manner, and is situated in one of the finest thoroughfares in the world. The price of admission is 6d. and 1s.; this includes afternoon tea from the hours of 3 to 7 p.m."

By 1910, the motion picture had become an integral part of Irish life. As an example of its popularity in Dublin, *The Bioscope* (July 8, 1909) reported that the proprietors of the Rotunda were fined ten pounds for permitting overcrowding during the film presentation of the Johnson-Burns fight on April 29 and 30 and May 1.

A vast number of short subjects on Ireland and on various aspects of Irish life began to appear at this time, dealing with everything from the animals in the Dublin zoo to the Irish cloth industry. On June 26, 1913, the General Film Company in the United Kingdom released a 330-foot subject, titled simply *Irish Life*. According to *The Bioscope* (June 12, 1913), it featured "amusing snapshots of Co. Kerry and its beauties, fetching turf, the famous cattle-fairs, some beasts being seen leaving a house in a short cut to the sheds. The famous Latigne Memorial, with its curious double engine, concludes a most interesting picture."

From the British company Kineto came the 365-foot *The Irish Cloth Industry* (released in the United Kingdom and Ireland on July 17, 1916). Kineto also released, on May 2, 1918, a 500-foot, or half-reel, subject showing a *Tank Training School in Ireland*. "This," commented *The Bioscope* (March 21, 1918), "is the first instance of a close-up cine camera display of a tank." *Leaves from Nature's Books, No. 3*, a 480-foot subject, released on November 23, 1916, by Davison's Film Sales Agency, featured "delightful studies of captive wild life, taken in the Dublin zoo."

In September 1915, Kineto filmed all the resorts in the South of Ireland for use for promotional purposes by the Tourist Development Association. According to *The Bioscope* (September 9, 1915), "the film, which depicts the journeyings of a tourist in the South, is quite a work of art." *The First Irish National Pilgrimage to Lourdes* was the subject of a two-reel film from the General Film Agency, released in the United States in January 1914. It showed a number of Irish citizens—Grace Maloney, Patrick Casey and Miss B.J. McDonogh—receiving miraculous cures at the French shrine.

Quite obviously, it was not going to be long before a producer recognized the commercial potential of a film version of the life of Ireland's patron saint. The first to realize St. Patrick's box-office value was one J. Theobold Walsh, whose organization, the Photo-Historic Film Company, released a three-reel production of *The Life of St. Patrick* in 1913. At the time he made the film,

Norman Whitten, 1919

Walsh was a resident of the United States, and may even have been an American citizen, but the opening title of the film, aside from assuring its viewers that the scenes were "taken upon the very grounds upon which St. Patrick trod," also announced that it was "directed by an Irishman."

An advertisement for the film in the British *The Moving Picture Offered List* (November 1, 1913) reads, "Highly endorsed by the Clergy.... A perfect presentation of an Historical Masterpiece. No expenses spared in the production. Every scene taken on the exact spot made memorable by Ireland's Apostle

Native Film Production

Lupita (Alice Keating) is a slave girl sold with St. Patrick in Norman Whitten's *In the Days of St. Patrick*. One thousand local artists appeared in the film.

and enacted by Irish peasants in Ancient Historical Costumes." The production was reviewed in the United States by *The Moving Picture World* on October 25, 1913, at which time it was released on a states rights basis by Phil P. Benedict:

> Overlooking some inconsequential defects in the photography there is much in this picture to interest that class of the American public who are concerned in subjects of a distinctly Roman Catholic nature. How true the events in the life of Saint Patrick are the scenes depicted can only be conjectured, yet they possess interest and, furthermore, they are said to have been taken in Ireland near the points believed to have been frequented by the saintly man during life. Many interesting views of Ireland are given.

Niall (T. O'Carroll Reynolds), standing with whip, brings Patrick in chains to Ireland.

> This subject should have staple value for rental to Roman Catholic Societies. As a matter of fact, it has been highly applauded by members of a number of such societies in and near New York to whom it has been shown.

Variety (April 11, 1913) announced that Walsh was planning to return to Ireland in May 1913 to produce further historical subjects, but there is no evidence that such films were either completed or released.

A far more important production on the life of St. Patrick was Norman Whitten's 1920 work, *In the Days of St. Patrick*. Whitten had commenced his film career in 1898 as the first male employee of pioneer British filmmaker Cecil Hepworth. He photographed Hepworth's *Rescued by Rover* (1905), which is to Britain what *The Great Train Robbery* is to American cinema. In 1910, with his wife, May Clark, he moved to Dublin and formed the General Film Supply Company. With J. Gordon Lewis as his cameraman, Whitten filmed and released a variety of short subjects dealing with Irish life and society. In 1917, he introduced Ireland's first newsreel, *Irish Events*, and also produced two films which were obviously little more than advertising items, *Matchmaking in Ireland*, filmed at Patterson's Match Factory, Hammond Lane, Dublin, and *The Court Film*, showing the work of the Court Laundry. In December 1918, Whitten produced Ireland's first animated film, *Ten Days Leave*, one half-reel in length, drawn by Irish artist Frank Leah, and photographed by J. Gordon Lewis. The short was first seen at the Bohemian Theatre, Dublin.

Interior scenes for *In the Days of St. Patrick* were filmed in a converted office on Dublin's Brunswick Street (now Pearse Street). St. Patrick was played as a ten-year-old by Whitten's son, Vernon, as a 16-year-old by Gilbert Green, and as an adult by Ira Allen. Others in the cast included Mrs. Alice Cardinall (as Patrick's mother), Dermot McCarthy (as Patrick's father), Alice Keating (as Patrick's sister, Lupita), Herbert Mayne (as Gormias), T. O'Carroll Reynolds (as Niall), and "Cyclone" Billy Warren, a black boxer who had settled in Dublin, and was a well known character in his later years. Norman Whitten directed, and J. Gordon Lewis was the cinematographer. Exteriors were filmed chiefly in the Rush area of North County Dublin.

In the Days of St. Patrick (or to give it its Gaelic title, *Aimsir Padraig*) was released with titles in both English and Gaelic. The titles were designed by William J. Walsh, and the translations into Gaelic were by Richard O Foghludha (also known as Fiachra Eilgeach).

The film no longer survives, but the following detailed, reel-by-reel description is taken from a synopsis filed for copyright purposes with the Library of Congress:

> Part One: Shows some memorials of St. Patrick: his grave at Downpatrick, his Bell, the Pilgrims climbing, and at their devotion on Croagh Patrick in 1919; the Cathedral of St. Patrick at Armagh, and the present successor of the long line of Patrick's Comharbs, His Eminence Cardinal Logue, blessing the children of St. Patrick's "Children of Erin," in all lands and on all seas.
>
> Part Two: The child and his parents are shown to us. Cormias, though blind, administers baptism to St Patrick, from the waters of a well which miraculously springs up, and recovers his sight. At the age of ten years we find him with his sister Lupita at fosterage. He works his first miracle, making icicles burn like wood.
>
> Part Three: At 16 years he is captured by Irish raiders, brought to Ireland and sold to Milcho, by whom he is sent to herd swine on the mountains. He gives himself to prayer and learns the speech of his captors. After six years he escapes, and is directed by Victor how to proceed. The Roman traders know that as he is a Christian he is a Roman, and take him with them.
>
> Part Four: Back in the Roman land, he dreams of the Irish children and hears their voices calling him to return and tell them about God. He prepares for his mission at Marmoutier and is ordained in Rome by Pope Celestine.
>
> Part Five: He returns to Ireland, adopts the boy Benignus as his

spiritual offspring, and foretells he will succeed him in his apostolate. On his approach to the house of Milcho the hardened old pagan sets fire to his house and is burned with it. He makes his first important convert, Dichu, who gives him the famed Sabhall or Barn, the first Christian church in Erin.

Part Six: He now draws nigh to Tara, where the High King was holding festival. He lights his Paschal Fire on the summit of Slane Hill before the Druids had kindled the Beil Teine, or fire of Beal, and its fanning was the challenge of the Christian to the Pagan. The infuriated King summons Patrick before him. For some reason he gets a hearing. Lochru the druid dies. The Queen pays him homage. Another druid attempts to poison him in the Banquet Hall, but Patrick frustrates him and preaches to the Court. We next see him destroy the stronghold of idolatry at Magh Slech, and afterwards on Croagh Aighle during his fast of forty days. Finally, we see him in his traditional garb and role banishing the serpents, and on his bed of death.

In May 1920, Norman Whitten brought the film to New York, screening it for the National Board of Review, and arranging for its release through the Kelwin Film Company. The first New York presentation was a three-week run at the Lexington Theatre in January 1921. In a review, *The Moving Picture World* (January 22, 1921) commented, "The story has been simply and reverently handled with no attempt at the spectacular. The cast is composed entirely of amateurs, who volunteered their services, and considering the circumstances under which it was made it will undoubtedly prove satisfactory to the limited clientele to whom it is evidently intended to appeal. Its chief charm lies in its simplicity and sincerity. It is not a picture which will appeal to the average theatre audience."

The Kelwin Film Company appears to have specialized in the American release of films with Irish backgrounds. In January of 1921, it released a short subject titled *Ireland Today*, which dealt with the uprising leading to the establishment of the Irish Free State. *The Moving Picture World* (January 22, 1921) reported that the film was "sub-titled in such a manner that the picture will certainly not appeal to those who are inclined to side with the British government. In fact, it is clearly propaganda for the other side."

Norman Whitten also produced three features—*Casey's Millions*, *Wicklow Gold* and *Cruiskeen Lawn*—made by Irish Photoplays, Ltd. in 1922. The films were directed and scripted by John McDonagh, photographed by J. Moise, and are chiefly of interest because they featured the popular Irish comedian, Jimmy O'Dea. The most important of the three films was *Cruiskeen Lawn*, which starred Tom Moran, Barrett MacDonnell, Fred Jeffs, Chris Silvester, and Fay Sargent. It concerned a horse named Cruiskeen Lawn, which wins a race thanks to a drug called "The Elixir of Life." A pecunious Irish squire, Boyle Roche, backs the horse and thus wins the girl, Nora Blake.

The trade press was far from kind in its opinion of the production. *Variety* (February 4, 1925) commented,

This picture is not a joke.... It is announced as "an Irish story acted and directed in Ireland by Irish people for the picturegoers of the world, a tonic for jaded patrons who are clamoring for something different in photoplays." It is different from the majority of pictures seen within the last 10 years, in fact it could almost lower the existing record for the world's worst. It is a bad thing of amateur experiment. The producer, his name appears to be Macdonagh [sic], is responsible for everything, including the story. He probably "acts," but modesty compels him to refrain from acknowledging his guilt. The leading people do not share the modesty of the producer-author. They are all poor and amateurish. Even the chance to exploit the beautiful scenery of the Emerald Isle has been studiously avoided.

"The settings are dull, uninteresting and entirely lacking in Irish character," reported *The Bioscope* (December 4, 1924). "The title of the film is uninspired and could readily be improved upon. We fear that *Cruiskeen Lawn* will prove entertaining to extremely unsophisticated audiences only." Similarly, the other British trade paper, *The Kinematograph Weekly* (December 4, 1924) commented, "The technical qualities are mediocre.... Only exterior sets are used which depict gardens in the characters' homes... the racecourse scene has little thrill."

Whether because of reviews such as these or because of the Civil War which followed the establishment of the Irish Free State in 1921, Norman Whitten left Ireland and returned to the British film industry. He retired in the late thirties, and died, at the age of 88, on June 3, 1969.

In 1915, C.A. McEvoy, the proprietor of the Masterpiece Theatre, Talbot Street, Dublin, became involved in production. In February, McEvoy had offered a prize of three guineas for the best Irish comedy suitable for film production, to run not more than 1,000 feet and to consist of no more than 25 scenes. The winning film, *Finglas Fair Day*, played entirely by amateurs, was released in June by McEvoy's Banba Company. Irish historian Proinsias O. Conluainn refers to a film from this period titled *Fun in a Finglas Fair*, which must presumably be this production. He cites F.J. McCormick as the leading player, but I have the assurance of McCormick's widow, Eileen Crowe, that he never appeared in such a film.

The ever-enterprising McEvoy also filmed *The Children's Folk Dancing Fete* in Phoenix Park, Dublin, on June 5. Early in October, he organized a Charlie Chaplin competition film, in which appeared a number of local Chaplin imitators. The audience at the Masterpiece selected the best performance.

The most important native Irish film production company, the Film Company of Ireland, was active during the latter half of the teens decade. It was created by an Irish-American lawyer, James Mark Sullivan, in the same year as the Easter Rebellion in Dublin, 1916. Sullivan's efforts were less abortive than those of Padraig Pearse and his followers, and the Film Company of Ireland survived for more than a year.

The earliest of the films to be produced by the Film Company of Ireland was *O'Neil of the Glens*, directed by Henry Fitzgibbon. The film was screened at the Bohemian Theatre, Dublin, late in July 1916, and, as the audience entered, it was photographed by a cameraman from the Film Company of Ireland. The footage was later screened as an addition to the program, probably ensuring that audiences returned for a second time in the hopes of viewing themselves on the screen.

On November 16, 1916, *The Bioscope* announced that the Film Company of Ireland was ceasing production until the next February "owing to poor light." Henry Fitzgibbon departed for the United States, but it was reported he would return in the spring and open a permanent studio for the company at Ringsend, Dublin.[1]

In the meantime, three one-reel Film Company of Ireland productions were released in the United Kingdom by Davison's Film Sales Agency Ltd.: *Widow Malone* (released January 15, 1917), *An Unfair Love Affair* (released January 22, 1917) and *A Romance of Puck Fair* (released January 29, 1917). Of the first, *The Bioscope* (December 14, 1916) commented, "Irish comedy, well acted, and the photography much improved. These Irish film players deserve to succeed, and, with a little more care in studio setting and a little more experience with the camera, they will assuredly do so."

The release of these films tends to minimize a report in the January 1917 issue of the Irish trade paper, *Irish Limelight*, that the first three months of the Film Company of Ireland's work had been wiped out in a Dublin fire. However, the Film Company of Ireland was facing problems. Fitzgibbon, as beforementioned, was out of the country, and, in June 1917, a petition for the winding up of the company was presented to the British Courts of Chancery. At that time it was reported that it had sustained a loss of £1,526.

Despite setbacks, the Film Company of Ireland continued its work. In April 1917, it released the four-reel *A Girl of Glenbeigh*, featuring Kathleen O'Connor. In June 1917, *Irish Limelight* reported that, "There are great possibilities before the Film Company of Ireland. It is to be hoped that they will realise them. Personally I believe they will. They are a good crowd, good actors and good fellows every one of them."

William Moser, formerly with the Pathé Company, had been named head cameraman and general manager early in 1917, and the first film upon which he worked was *Rafferty's Rise*, released in the fall of 1917, starring Fred Donovan as Constable Rafferty, supported by Brian McGowan, Miss K. Murphy, Brenda Burke, and Arthur Shields. "The film was typically Irish," commented *Irish Limelight* (November 1917). "The humor is clean and healthy, and of the most original type, the setting is the beautiful scenery of the Dublin mountains, and the photography is as good as, if not better than, anything I have yet seen. The actors and actresses, too, were adapted to the parts they portrayed."

The most important of the Film Company of Ireland productions was

Knocknagow, adapted by Mrs. N.F. Patton from the popular (and still in print) novel by Charles Kickham. Initially some nine reels (8,700 feet) in length, the film appears to have been eventually released as a six-reel production. It featured Fred O'Donovan (who also directed), Nora Clancey, Valentine Roberts, Kathleen Murphy, Arthur Shields, Brian McGowan, Alice Keating, Kathleen O'Connor, and Cyril Cusack.

From 1911 onwards, the great Irish actor Micheál Mac Liammóir (1899-1978) had appeared on the British stage and in British films as Alfred Willmore, which is his name in its English form. His first screen appearance as Micheál Mac Liammóir was in *Knocknagow*. "What my part was, I cannot imagine!" he wrote, "probably the Idiot Boy."[2]

Nora Clancey, who was married to Fred O'Donovan, was a member of the Abbey Theatre Company and her presence in Film Company of Ireland productions was considered something of a coup for the organization. In a February 1917 interview with *Irish Limelight*, she said of her film work, "I was not particularly affected by the absence of an audience and the applause. I think the main difficulty encountered by the beginner is the necessarily limited space in which one has to work in the studio. I always felt that I would find it difficult to avoid watching the camera operator, but in this I was wrong. I might mention that in film work all gestures and the like must be reduced to the absolute minimum; practically only natural movements can be tolerated."

Knocknagow was trade shown on February 6, 1918, at the Sackville Street Picture House. Its first public performance took place at Magner's Cinema Clonmel—the film had been shot in the area—on January 30, 1918. The manager of the theatre wired this report to the Film Company of Ireland at its offices at 34 Dame Street, Dublin: "*Knocknagow* a terrific success. All records smashed. Packed solid before advertised hour. Waiting crowds necessitated police supervision. Heartiest congratulations on film which is a credit to yourselves and to Ireland."[3]

The story of *Knocknagow*, set in the Ireland of the 1850s, concerns Arthur O'Connor, who gives up the notion of becoming a priest because he has fallen in love with Mary Kearney. The general theme is the oppression of Irish peasants by absentee English landlord Sir Garrett Butler. The suggestion of Irish nationalism was very apparent in titles such as "In the name of the law that protects you [the English agent], the huts are pulled down that the people may perish; there will be an awful reckoning, if not in our time then later," "It's a land of plenty, and God forgive those who come to Ireland to starve the Irish," and "What curse is on an Irishman that he cannot have even poverty's crumb for his dear ones?"

The film opened in England and was reviewed by *The Bioscope* (October 16, 1919), which noted, "There is more than a soupçon of underlying propaganda about this native Irish production, which, although it has many technical faults, is by no means without charm and interest.... If *Knocknagow* is carefully edited it can be made a production of considerable interest, but it obviously needs thorough revision." Sometime later, *The Bioscope* (on January 15, 1920) took a second look at the film and commented, it "is, to say the least, nothing to get excited over." Irish-American audiences were, perhaps rightly, more enthusiastic. *The Boston Globe*—one hopes not in all seriousness— wrote, "The best photography we have seen in any European picture to date is in *Knocknagow*. The acting is remarkable for its naturalness and the Irish pictures have surely won a place in the American markets on their merits."

Other Film Company of Ireland productions from 1917 include *When Love Comes to Gavin, Burke, The Miser's Gift, Woman's Wit, Food of Love, The Eleventh Hour*, and twenty reels of scenic shorts.

The last important Film Company of Ireland feature was *Willy Reilly and His Colleen Bawn*, based on the novel by William Carleton, and starring Brian McGowan, Frances Alexander and Jim Plant. The film was concerned with an eighteenth century love affair between a Catholic gentleman and a Protestant heiress. Promotional material from the time of the film's initial release comments: "The reciprocal acts of goodwill by both Catholics and Protestants throughout the play beautifully illustrates the moral of national brotherhood, and demonstrates the truth, so often forgotten, that men may worship their God at different altars while serving their common country side by side."[4]

Willy Reilly and His Colleen Bawn was directed by John McDonough, from County Tipperary, who had first become involved with the motion picture by writing a scenario for the 1910 American Biograph production, *The Fugitive*, while living and working in the United States. Around the time he completed *Willy Reilly and His Colleen Bawn*, McDonough made a film promoting the Irish Republican Loan, in front of Padraig Pearse's St. Edna's School—where portions of *Willy Reilly and His Colleen Bawn* were shot—and utilizing a table supposedly associated with Robert Emmett during his courtship with Sarah Curran. "In those dangerous and exciting times," recalled McDonough, "No cinema owner would dare risk exhibiting the Republican Loan films so it was planned for a few volunteers in fast cars to visit certain cinemas, rush the operator's box, and, at gun-point, force the operator to take off the film he was showing, and put on the Loan film."[5]

Although it might be supposed that politics involved the films themselves rather than the theatres in which they were screened, Irish theatres were not immune from the aftermath of political protest. The Grand Cinema, on Sackville Street, was burnt down during the Easter Rebellion. Its proprietor, William Kay, took over control of the Rotunda, with Ernest Jameson, and brought the Grand Cinema Orchestra with him. In November 1926, armed men entered the Masterpiece Cinema, Dublin, and seized a copy of the film *Ypres*, which glorified the British army during the First World War. When the Masterpiece Cinema insisted on continuing to screen the film, the theatre was blown up.

However, political or terrorist acts were minor problems compared with moral censorship restrictions placed upon Irish theatres. The Public Health Committee had appointed W. Butler and Councillor P. Lennon as Dublin's film censors in the summer of 1916. Their mission was to order theatre managers to remove any section of a film which might injure the morals of the Irish public. In July 1917, Father Farrell read a paper to the Dublin Vigilance Association on "The Dangerous Influence of Picture Houses." The Right Reverend Monsignor Dunne noted that he had "yet to visit a picture theatre at which some objectionable subject was not screened."[6]

The Roman Catholic Church's control of film exhibition and, to a lesser extent, production in Ireland, even during the period of British rule, was considerable. The 1914 American production of *Neptune's Daughter*, directed by Irish-born Herbert Brenon, and starring — with surprisingly little in the way of clothing — Annette Kellermann, was scheduled to be shown at the Sandford Cinema on July 22, 1915. The previous Sunday it was denounced by the local priest, with the result, as noted in *The Bioscope* (July 29, 1915), that "scores could not obtain admission." When the Selig Polyscope Company's 1916 production of *The Garden of Allah* eventually reached Ireland in 1918, through the Dublin-based National Films, Ltd., the company's proprietor, N. Ormsby-Scott, was required to screen the production for Cannon O'Connell, representing the Archbishop of Dublin. Much concern was expressed over the hero's being referred to as Father Antoine, implying that he was an ordained priest. It was requested that the film's titles be changed to "Brother," thus making the leading man only a renegade monk.[7]

Formal film censorship began in Ireland in 1924. The previous year, representatives of the Irish Vigilance Association, the Priest Social Guild, the Social Reform Committee and various church groups had met with Kevin O'Higgins, Minister for Home Affairs, and he introduced the Censorship of Films Act, which was passed in June 1923. W.B. Yeats spoke out against the act, arguing that he wished to "leave the arts superior or inferior to the general conscience of mankind." The act provided for a censor to refuse certification to films which were "indecent, blasphemous or obscene." According to Kevin Rockett, in his detailed study of film censorship in Ireland, in its first year of operation, 104 films were banned and a further 166 were cut.[8]

To those with even a modicum of intelligence, Irish film censorship and its history are a source of continuing amusement. Because the censor had no sound projector in the first year of the talkies in Ireland, he was unable to listen to the soundtracks of any of the submitted films, with the result that certificates were issued with the legend "Plot and Sound Not Censored." It was not until 1930 that a bill was passed giving the censor power to censor what could be heard as well as seen.

Films with homosexual overtones, such as Roman Polanski's *Knife in the Water* (1962), were passed for exhibition because it was argued that the average Irishman had no knowledge of homosexuality, and what he did not understand would not harm him. The Marx Brothers' feature *Monkey Business* (1931) was banned because it might lead to anarchy. *The Great Dictator* (1940) was banned, as was Noel Coward's *Brief Encounter* (1945). Eisenstein's *Potemkin* (1925) could not be shown publicly, and its presentation in the Republic was limited to Film Society of Ireland screenings. *Gone with the Wind* (1939) was heavily cut for Irish consumption. Appropriate title changes were made to coincide with religious beliefs; for example *I Want a Divorce* (1940) was released in Ireland as *The Tragedy of Divorce*.

Major changes in film censorship occurred with the creation of the Censorship of Films Appeal Board in 1965, although an appeals board had operated since the inception of film censorship. Films continue to be rated and censored as to the age of the audience, although, more and more, there is a move afoot for the end of censorship of films for adult audiences only.

The twenties could not compare to the previous decade in the quantity of Irish filmmaking, nor, might it be added, did they herald any increase in quality. The decade opened with a mild flurry of interest in Ireland as a good location for film production. "Pat" of Dublin wrote to the popular British fan magazine, *Pictures and the Picturegoer* (February 1922), "Now that there's peace in old Ireland once more, I hope movie-makers will get busy and let us have some Irish pictures. We have unrivalled scenic backgrounds and everyone knows that our Irish girls are the finest in the world."

Another British film magazine, *Picture Plays*, published a piece extolling the virtues of Killarney as a new Los Angeles:

> The natural "home" of the film in Britain is Ireland—the country of romance, scenery and sunshine—with, perhaps, Killarney as the centre.... The air of Ireland is the cleanest to be found in Western Europe, and the days on which "exterior" work would be possible during the year is nearly double the average number in England. The material for "plots," too, is there in plenty. The countryside teems with literary associations, and practically every village has been immortalised by some romance.... The day that Ireland is "discovered" will be a red-letter day for the British film, for it will give to us what we have lacked too long—a great film centre which will supply all the needs, both of scenery and climate, of all the films we can produce.[9]

There was some British film production in Ireland in the late 'teens. *Rock of Ages* (1918), directed by Bertram Phillips and starring Queenie Thomas and Kenelm Foss, was filmed there. In 1919, the British company Regal Films produced a six-reel version of the popular Irish ballad *Father O'Flynn*. Ralph Forster appeared in the title role, supported by Eileen Bellamy, "Little Rex" (a child actor), Ethel Douglas, Eric Harrison, Tom Coventry, and Reginald Fox. The film was written and directed by Tom Watts, and photographed by J.C. Bee Mason.

Interior scenes were shot in England, but the majority of the exteriors were photographed in Ireland. The use of the Irish locations was a heavy factor in promoting the production, as the following quote from contemporary publicity indicates: "It was taken in and around the beauty spots of Erin's finest scenery—the Lakes of Killarney. There with some of Nature's lovliest shrines for backgrounds, you can see developed one of the most human stories that has ever been presented on the printed page or the kinema screen."

The English *Daily Mail* critic noted "the delightful glimpses of life amongst the Irish peasantry, and of Killarney's winding streams and woodland dells." *The Bioscope* (July 31, 1919), in a lengthy review, commented, "The outstanding feature of this straightforward, conventional little Irish love drama is the exquisite beauty of the real Irish scenery against which most of the action passes.... The film concludes with a series of *tableaux vivants* presenting wonderful gems of Killarney scenery. Their beauty is so great that one can afford to overlook the fact that they are somewhat long-drawn out and lacking in dramatic value. Some cutting would, however, improve several of the earlier episodes."

A number of British films with Irish themes or stories were produced by the British film industry in the twenties. Stoll produced a feature based on George A. Birmingham's novel, *General John Regan* (directed by Harold Shaw and starring Milton Rosmer and Madge Stuart), in 1921. When the film was eventually screened in Dublin at the Metropole Theatre in the fall of 1922, it created a minor controversy in the pages of the *Irish Independent* after the Reverend J.F. Flavin protested,

> I availed myself of the earliest opportunity of seeing the production in the cinema and was horrified to think that such a travesty of Irish character and Irish life should be shown in the heart of Ireland. It is, indeed, nauseating for any self-respecting Irishman to see in the city of Dublin a film of Irish life in which the principal characters were pigs, the main scenery dirt, the chief characteristics of the people quarrelling, fighting, ignorance, drunkenness, sloth, and lying intrigue, with the representative of the Catholic Church an acquiescing buffoon. Imagine this film being advertised in a foreign country as being "eminently successful in Dublin" and you can readily realise why we are sometimes slandered as "the dirty, ignorant Irish."

Dion Boucicault's *The Colleen Bawn* was filmed in 1923 by Stoll. Released as a seven-reel feature in May 1924, the film was directed by W.P. Kellino, and featured Henry Victor, Stewart Rome and Marie Ault. "The pleasant Irish atmosphere of this old melodrama is well conveyed in this screen version," reported *The Kinematograph Weekly* (January 31, 1924). The play was again filmed by a British company, Twickenham Studios, in 1934, under the title *Lily of Killarney*. The new version was directed by Maurice Elvey and featured Stanley Holloway, Dorothy Boyd, John Garrick, and Gina Malo. Apart from a prologue showing views of the Killarney area, the film was shot entirely in England.

On August 27, 1921, *The Moving Picture World* announced:

> A series of photoplays based on Irish life and character, Irish history and sentiment of the past, will be presented by Celtic Photoplays, Inc. It is stated that these pictures will have competent direction, casting and acting, and will show the country as it really is and not as its people are frequently presented in comic songs or on the vaudeville stage. For instance, they will show Ireland as a country of art, science, literature, poetry, music and drama and what the world owes it along these lines.

Nothing appears to have come of these plans, but a year earlier a company with a similar name, the Celtic Film Company, had been established in Dublin. It produced one feature, a four-reel adaptation of John Denvers' play, *Rosaleen Dhu*, released in the United Kingdom on March 17, 1920. The story dealt with evicted tenants and absentee landlords and, although chiefly set in Connemara, Galway, also took place in Algeria. However, as *The Kinematograph Weekly* (February 5, 1920) commented, "It is the Irish atmosphere which will get the film over if anything can, but it must be admitted that it failed to inspire the actors. There were opportunities for introducing little humorous bits that would have helped the picture along, but no advantage was taken of these. From the production point of view there was a lack of that attention to detail which people expect nowadays, although certainly very pretty country has been chosen for the Irish scenes." *Rosaleen Dhu* was directed by William J. Powers, who also portrayed the villainous Malone. Sadly, Powers died, accidentally, in the same year as the film was released.

In 1924, John Hurley produced a romantic drama titled *Land of Her Fathers*, which featured Phyllis Wakely, Barry Fitzgerald, Maureen Delaney, and Micheál Mac Liammóir. The last recalled,

> Phyllis Wakely, as far as I know, was not a professional actress, but a very talented Trinity [College] girl, extremely pretty and a true daughter of the 20's. I have still, or rather my manager Brian Tobin, has, and guards it like his life, a still of Phyllis and myself which is an amusing period piece; I, gazing rapturously at her as she sits in dangerous proximity to Power's Waterfall, in full cocktail regalia of the mid-twenties — cloche hat, white fox edged skirt, and what appears to be ballroom shoes and all!
> Frank Hugh O'Donnell had a great deal to do with the film, and I think played a small part in it; the company was an American one headed by a Mr. Sullivan. The cameraman, whose name I have forgotten, was an extremely competent and a very nice fellow, also American. The late Tom Moran also played in the picture, and a few others, all of whom have vanished from my memory and probably from the surface of the earth, although Phyllis Wakely is very much alive and married to somebody in England. She came to see me in my dressing room one night in London about four years ago [1964].[10]

The last Irish-produced silent feature was *Irish Destiny*, directed and written by Dr. I.J. Eppel, proprietor of the Palace Cinema (now the Academy), Dublin. The film was photographed by British cinematographer Joe Rosenthal, and featured Desmond O'Shea (as a volunteer), Mary Connor (as his mother), Michael Dempsey (as his father), Una Shiels (as a schoolteacher), Valentine Vousden (as a priest), Kit O'Malley (as an IRA captain), Cathal McGarvey (as a Jolly Jarvey), Peggy O'Rorke (as his daughter), and Brian McGowan (as a villain).

A glorification of the activities of the Irish Republican Army in the war of independence, *Irish Destiny* utilizes stock footage of English troops in Dublin, the Black and Tans, and the burning of Cork. It also preached against illegal whiskey stills, pointing out that poteen is "a vile and ruinous alcoholic concoction, the distilling of which is prohibited by the Irish Republican Army." Scenes were filmed at the "Meeting of the Waters," Vaughan's Hotel, Dublin (headquarters of the IRA), and on O'Connell Street (taken from the back of a motorbike). The film features a reenactment of the escape of 200 prisoners from the Curragh Internment Camp, and the American version ends, for no apparent reason, with shots of a New York St. Patrick's Day Parade, with the Irish dancers shown at quickened speed.[11] *Variety* (April 13, 1927) commented,

> This may be *The Big Parade* and *What Price Glory* of the Irish cinema, but it is doubtful whether its appeal will interest others than those from the ould sod.... Dr. Eppel, who scenarized and produced the film with a cast of actors recruited from the various theatre movements of Ireland, has adhered strictly to history of the Irish combat, weaving only the required love interest into proceedings. But withal he has succeeded only in grinding out a picture with class instead of public appeal.... From a melodramatic angle the battle scenes are well reproduced and a coherent love story sustained of a boy who upon his wedding eve enlists with the Republican army and does himself proud. The film's local future lies in auspices, tie-ups with Irish societies, etc. As a general release it cannot get far because of its limited appeal.

The sound film came to Ireland on April 21, 1929, with the opening of the Al Jolson vehicle *The Singing Fool* at the Capitol Cinema, Dublin. However, there was one more important silent film to be made in Ireland and that was the four-reel *Guests of the Nation*, produced by the Gate Theatre in 1934, directed by playwright Denis Johnston (best known for *The Moon in the Yellow River* and *The Old Lady Says No*), edited by Mairin Hayes, and with a scenario by Mary Manning and continuity by Geoffrey Dalton, from the short story by Frank O'Connor. O'Connor appeared in the film playing a small role, and leading parts were taken by Barry Fitzgerald and Cyril Cusack.

Shot on 16mm, the film is somewhat amateurish in its use of a hand-held camera, the over-use of reflectors (particularly at the end of the second reel), and the melodramatic lighting of some sequences, notably the trial. It is, however, a noble attempt by Johnston, who certainly has a visual style and manages to convey the helplessness of the two IRA men ordered to murder two British soldiers in revenge for the execution of two IRA men held by the British. *Guests of the Nation* was not the only 16mm production to achieve

A dramatic moment from *Irish Destiny*.

some renown in Ireland in the early thirties; in August 1930, the Peacock Theatre screened Mary Manning's *Bank Holiday* and Norris Davidson's *By Accident*. Davidson was influenced by Flaherty's *Man of Aran*, and a few years later produced a 16mm documentary on a dance peculiar to the Aran Islands, and titled *Damhsa Arann*.

The first Irish sound film is generally credited to be *The Voice of Ireland*, which was apparently produced in 1932, although it was certainly not seen outside of Ireland until 1936. Directed by Colonel Victor Haddick, the film featured Haddick, along with Richard Hayward and Barney O'Hara, and was little more than a travelogue with a slim storyline involving a returned Irish exile visiting the scenes of his youth. It was very much a middle-class, Anglo-Irish view of the new country. Released in the United Kingdom by International Cine, *The Voice of Ireland* was some 4,400 feet in length. It was reviewed on April 2, 1936 by *The Kinematograph Weekly*:

> An attempt has been made to give a kind of sequence to the exterior shots, which range from views of lakes and mountains to fox-hunting, horsebreeding and folk-dancing. Even one or two scenes in ancient Ireland have been reconstructed, but half-heartedly and with obvious economy.
> When a close-up of a singer or instrumentalist is required, the performer is made-up in a way suggesting the crudest amateur theatricals. The commentary is delivered in an Irish brogue which lends authenticity,

but both sound effects and background music are lacking, and pauses in the commentary leave a dead silence even when motor-racing is on the screen. Recording is generally harsh.

The one studio setting is obviously artificial, or the "two-flats" variety, and the photography in general suggests an enthusiastic amateur on his holidays.

Richard Hayward was involved with Donovan Pedelty in a series of "Irish" films produced in the mid-thirties. The two men were both from Northern Ireland, and Hayward acted as leading man and sometime producer, with Pedelty serving as director and screenwriter.

The first "Irish" film which the two men made was *Luck of the Irish* (1935), which co-starred Kay Walsh and Niall MacGinnis, and was released by Paramount-British. The story was melodramatic, but Hayward contributed a number of songs, and the film was good enough to gain an American release, opening at New York's 47th Street Cinema on January 15, 1936. *Variety* (January 20, 1936) commented, "With a little of the proverbial Celtic good fortune and the application of a soft pedal on the fact that the cast and story are both indigenous to northern Ireland, this all–Irish film should do well among the sons of Erin. Since most of the Irish comes from the southern Catholic three-quarters of the isle, and the animosity toward the upper eastern corner is w.k., knowledge of the film's origin won't help."

Luck of the Irish was followed by *Irish and Proud of It* (1936), which was eventually released in the United States in 1938. It featured Hayward as an Irish singer who makes his living in London, where he expresses a desire to return to his home village of Ballyvoraine in Northern Ireland. Members of the Irish Flying Club make his wish a reality by kidnapping him and flying him to the village, where Hayward becomes involved in a fight with an ex–Chicago gangster. Dinah Sheridan was featured as "a pretty young Irish colleen" in love with a member of the mobster's gang (played by Liam Gaffney). "The real Irish wit and the genuineness of the characters and the scenery make up for the unprofessional touches of the production," reported *The Film Daily* (November 7, 1938).

The final "Irish" feature from Pedelty and Hayward was *The Early Bird*, also released in the United Kingdom by Paramount-British in 1936, but which does not appear to have been seen in the United States. Based on a play by Tom Carnduff presented at the Belfast Repertory Theatre, *The Early Bird* told of a revolt by villagers against a puritanical woman. Unlike the two earlier films, it did not have the benefit of a "name" actress to play opposite Hayward.

Both Hayward and Pedelty continued to make films together, sometimes with Scottish backgrounds. Pedelty's career as a screenwriter and director lasted from 1933 through 1939. Richard Hayward died in a car crash near Belfast on October 13, 1964, at the age of seventy-two. His last screen appearance was in the 1958 British feature *A Night to Remember*.

Hayward and Pedelty were not the only production team making so-called Irish films during this period. A number of British features had Irish themes and settings. In 1934, Columbia-British released *Sweet Inniscara*, directed and written by Emmett Moore, and featuring Sean Rogers and Mae Ryan. *The Kinematograph Weekly* (February 22, 1934) was not impressed:

> The Irish scenery and folk songs contained in the picture might have been adapted into an interesting short, but are lost sight of in the crude story. Production and acting are on the lowest amateur level. Appeal is to exhibitors of local halls or to those curious about one of the first Irish talkies. "By what witchcraft has he ensnared my daughter?" and "I will not sign the contract until the clock has struck the hour" are fair samples of the stilted dialogue. Story is padded out with scenes and songs which have nothing to do with the action.

Slightly better reviews awaited *Irish for Luck*, directed by Arthur Woods, and released by Warner Bros.–British in 1936. The film featured Patric Knowles, Margaret Lockwood and Athene Seyler.

One major British director who began his career with Irish features and who had been born in Castle Reagh, Ireland, on February 12, 1900 was Brian Desmond Hurst. A director responsible for many entertaining features such as *Dangerous Moonlight* (released in the United States as *Suicide Squadron*) and *Scrooge* (released in the United States as *A Christmas Carol*), Brian Desmond Hurst had worked at one time in the late twenties as an assistant to John Ford in Hollywood. Indeed his films have something of the visual qualities which make Ford's films so appealing.

One of Hurst's first productions was *Irish Hearts* (1934), which starred Lester Matthews, Molly Lamont and Patric Knowles, together with a number of players from the Abbey Theatre, headed by Arthur Sinclair, Sara Allgood and her sister, Máire O'Neill. The silly, melodramatic story concerned a doctor with insufficient income to marry the nurse, Norah O'Neale, whom he loves. The film was released in the United States, late in 1934, under the title of *Norah O'Neale*, and American critics were not particularly impressed. *Variety* (October 30, 1934) had to admit that it was "badly cut, slow and jumpy." In the *New York Times* (October 25, 1934), Andre Sennwald described it as "So deficient technically as to embarrass the visitor who is lured to it by the promise of an Irish-made photoplay with Irish players.... The drama is laboriously developed, the direction is painfully bad and the work betrays the fumbling hand of the amateur everywhere." New York exhibitors were further hampered in their efforts to promote the film by an injunction forbidding them to use the term "Abbey Players."

Irish Hearts was followed a year later by *Riders to the Sea*, based on the 1904 one-act play by John Millington Synge. It featured Sara Allgood and Ria Mooney, and was co-produced by the popular British Music Hall star Gracie Fields. Although she does not discuss the film in her 1961 autobiography *Sing as We Go*, Miss Fields does write affectionately of the two men responsible for her involvement in the film, writer Henry Savage and artist John Flanagan. She describes them as the "two men who completed my education, gave me the courage of my own common sense, and altered the whole of my life." They were also the men to whom credit should go for bringing the project to fruition, with Flanagan serving as Fields' co-producer.

The third of Hurst's early Irish features was *Ourselves Alone* (1936), which dealt with the 1921 battles between the Royal Irish Constabulary and the Irish Republican Army. The film featured John Lodge, John Loder, Antoinette Cellier, Niall MacGinnis, and Clifford Evans, and was first seen in the United States at New York's 55th Street Playhouse on July 30, 1937. "It emerges under Desmond Hurst's direction and the competent performances of its cast as one of the better things of its kind," wrote Frank S. Nugent in the *New York Times* (July 31, 1937). Hurst was so pleased with the American response to the film that he took out an advertisement in *Daily Variety*, in which he reprinted the review from *Variety* and added the comment, "With gratitude to my friend and mentor John Ford . . . sincerely, Brian Desmond Hurst."

Hurst returned to Irish themes briefly in 1942 with the wartime documentary *A Letter from Ulster*. In 1946, he made *Hungry Hill*, starring Margaret Lockwood and Dennis Price, and which is chiefly memorable for the performance of F.J. McCormick. Based on the novel by Daphne Du Maurier, the film is concerned with a feud between the Brodricks and the Donovans over a copper mine on Hungry Hill in Queen Victoria's Ireland. "Brian Desmond Hurst's direction, like the plot, is dramatically effective on occasion, and he achieves a number of interesting characterizations," reported *Newsweek* (November 10, 1947). Jesse Zunser was less kind in the New York entertainment weekly *Cue* (October 25, 1947). He called the film "an involved, interminably long and painfully tiresome tale of family feuds."

Brian Desmond Hurst was the first to film a play by Synge (1871–1909). For his final screen work he returned again to the playwright, with a superior film version of his 1907 play *The Playboy of the Western World*. Siobhan McKenna was cast as Pegeen Mike, with English actor Gary Raymond as Christy Mahon. In the *New York Times* (March 19, 1963), Bosley Crowther called the production "a ripe and rousing film," but most American critics were less enthusiastic. "Siobhan McKenna, for all her gloriously peat-boggy voice and her fine face with its mouth shaped like a shamrock leaf, is 20 years too old to be playing the fiery-tempered Pegeen opposite the likes of bhoyish Gary Raymond," commented *Time* (March 24, 1963). Most critical was Stanley Kauffmann in *The New Republic* (March 30, 1963):

> Nothing about the production compensates. Brian Desmond Hurst has directed dully. Even the outdoor scenes seem static. The camera focusses on the slope of a sand dune; then two characters come over the top of the dune and sit in the center of the focus. Simple details are slovenly; inside

the tavern we see through the open doorway that the sky has a wrinkle in it. The cast is mediocre, with Niall MacGinnis the best as mad Old Mahon. Siobhan McKenna is considered by some a great actress; to me she is sometimes a satisfactory one. Here she again leaves me unstirred, with her obvious and somewhat labored efforts, her heavy unexpressive features. Additionally Pegeen Mike is supposed to be "a wild-looking but fine girl of about twenty." Miss McKenna looks no more wild than, alas, she looks twenty; she seems the coeval of the Widow Quin, which badly unbalances the drama. In another curious piece of casting, Gary Raymond, an English actor, plays Christy and is so worried about his Irish accent, which keeps wearing thin, that he has little ebullience and vigor.

Brian Desmond Hurst died in London on September 26, 1986. His work in Irish cinema is largely forgotten, and, indeed, his obituary in *Daily Variety* spoke largely of *Dangerous Moonlight* (released in the United States in 1941 as *Suicide Squadron*), which starred Anton Walbrook as a Polish pianist, and ignored Hurst's other achievements.

What is generally regarded as the first true Irish sound feature is *The Dawn*, directed by Tom Cooper for his Hibernia Film Studios in a Killarney garage in 1936. Eight reels in length, *The Dawn* is concerned with a young man, Brian Malone (played by Brian O'Sullivan), who carries the stigma of his grandfather's being a traitor to the Fenian cause. Expelled from the IRA, Malone joins the Royal Irish Constabulary in disgust. However, he is able to save his IRA colleagues from the Black and Tans, and, after his brother Billy (played by Donal O'Cahill) is shot, it is revealed that Brian was expelled from the IRA not because of his grandfather but because Billy was an IRA intelligence officer and his presence in the group could have been an embarrassment.

Subtitled "Do Con Glóire dé Agus Onóire na H'Éireann" (To the Glory of God and the Honor of Ireland), *The Dawn* has a certain amateurish quality to it, particularly with regard to the acting, but it is not a film of which anyone involved should feel ashamed. *The Dawn* has a visual style and a panache in its direction which many a Hollywood filmmaker might envy. Cooper was also responsible for the screenplay, assisted by D.A. Moriarty and Donal O'Cahill. Other leading roles were played by Cooper (as Dan O'Donovan), Eileen Davis (as Eileen O'Donovan), Jerry O'Mahoney (as the Officer in Charge of the Black and Tans), Billy Murphy (as Sergeant Geary of the Royal Irish Constabulary), James Gleeson (as John Malone), and Marion O'Connell (as Mrs. Malone). Comic relief was provided by Herbert Martin (as Brassie) and Johnny McCarthy (as Johnny).

The film was first seen in Dublin at the Capitol Theatre on August 21, 1936. *The Irish Independent* (August 22, 1936) reported, "It was such a strong attraction that the receipts compared favorably with those recorded for other outstanding pictures. From start to finish the film held the attention of the audience, and bursts of applause showed the keen interest being taken in every scene."

The Dawn ran for three weeks at the Capitol, and was subsequently released in the United Kingdom by International Productions Limited. Reaction in the British trade press was less favorable than in Dublin. *The Kinematograph Weekly* (January 21, 1937) called the film "a crudely produced tale of turbulent times.... The players—all natives of Ireland—enter into the spirit of the thing with enthusiasm, but their histrionic abilities are far from adequate to the demands of the story.... The greatest claim of this film is authenticity, but apart from that the production is weak in every department.... Technically, the film lacks the polish to be found in the pictures of today. The quality of the photography fluctuates, and the interiors are cramped and badly lit. Dialogue, too, is almost inaudible at times." *The Monthly Film Bulletin* (January 1937) was a little more enthusiastic: "The acting is good, and so is much of the photography, but throughout the film is reminiscent of an amateur production. As such it is very good; as a professional production it is not so good."

The most enthusiastic response, although at times the comment reads as a backhanded compliment, came from *People* (January 17, 1937):

> The first ten minutes I said to myself: "Coo, lummy, what sort of tripe have I struck here?" It was too bad to be true. Then it started to grow on you, and another hour went by with the greatest of ease on the eye.
> Everybody did everything all wrong in modern film sense and technique, because they were all amateurs.
> If any one character had acted it would have spoiled the whole caboosh. Yet they all fitted in perfectly, even under the disadvantage of no makeup, in which all the men were dark-visaged and the women pale and wan.
> So you see it was a remarkable film. More remarkable its birth. One man took a chance, wrote it, created it, got together his own village cast, directed it, did everything on his own in Killarney. He bought all the material, paid all the expenses, customs duties and censorship fees and landed it in London.
> No twenty-five Czecho-Slovakian, Armenian and Greek-Americans to stage, film, direct, produce, sound-track, photograph, assistant photograph, etc., etc., as we are made to suffer before we are allowed to see any film nowadays.
> Just one man—a Tom Cooper—was them all. And it may make him a small fortune.
> Which is the real film romance at last.
> And, having seen it, I can say it is too bad to be true and too good to miss.

The Dawn was released in the United States in 1938 by William Alexander under the title of *Dawn over Ireland*. *The Film Daily* (February 19, 1938) reported, "As one of the pioneering efforts of the Emerald Isle, it is both credible and creditable entertainment, but it demonstrates that producers there have a long way to go in the mastery of the motion picture camera.... Irish audiences in particular will like this film."

Flushed with the success of *The Dawn*, Tom Cooper announced plans to form a partnership with Victor Haddick. The latter wrote a screenplay, *The Years Between*, which dealt with Wexford and Kerry history from 1798 to 1806, and Cooper planned to take six months on the film's production. The pair told *The Irish Press* (July 9, 1936) of their search for a new Irish girl "star," who was to be "an actress with Celtic beauty and fine histrionic powers."

Cooper's interest in filmmaking quickly waned, and he became involved in Killarney's best known occupation, that of tourism. In 1976, the National Film Studios presented him with a medal in honor of his contribution to the Irish film industry, and Cooper lived long enough to see *The Dawn* presented on Irish television. He died on May 17, 1982, in Tralee, at the age of eighty-two.

Few who had the privilege of watching Jimmy O'Dea (1900-1965) perform on stage will argue with the description of him in the London *Times* (January 8, 1965) as "Ireland's Greatest Comedian." His best known characterization was that of Biddy Mulligan, a Dublin scrubwoman. As with much of O'Dea's work, it was a creation which belonged to the Irish people; his performances could not particularly be translated to the non–Irish stage, and, thus, his appearances outside of the Republic were usually limited to centers of Irish immigration, such as Liverpool.

However, as already noted, O'Dea did appear in a number of films, two of the most prominent of which are *Blarney* (1938) and *Ireland's Border Line* (1939). The latter was released in the United States, opening at the Belmont Theatre, New York, a popular site for Irish-produced films of the sound era. Both films were directed by Harry O'Donovan, who wrote O'Dea's stage material from the twenties onwards. *Ireland's Border Line*, which also featured Noel Purcell, was concerned with the friendly rivalry between Northern Ireland and Ireland—probably the last film which was to find humor in the partition of Ireland. "Irish humor at its best makes this picture amusing and entertaining," reported *The Film Daily* (October 24, 1939). "There is an underlying effort in the story to point out the fact that both the north and south of Ireland are working for harmony, and will achieve it some day."

During the Second World War, Jimmy O'Dea gave a memorable performance as Bottom in a stage production of *A Midsummer Night's Dream* with Mícheál Mac Liammóir, and delighted audiences at Dublin's Gaiety Theatre with impersonations of Winston Churchill and Joseph Stalin. He returned to the screen in 1957, playing the railway porter in John Ford's *The Rising of the Moon*. His last screen appearance was in Walt Disney's 1959 production of *Darby O'Gill and the Little People*.

In 1938, the Irish National Film Corporation produced *Men of Ireland*, directed by John Duffy, and featured Cecil Ford, Brian O'Sullivan, Gabriel Fallon, and Gerard Duffy. Similar in concept to *Man of Aran*, the film was set on the Blasket Islands, and involved a medical student who falls in love with a native girl while on vacation. The native girl is loved by a local fisherman. The two men go out on a fishing trip, and the native lad is swept overboard, and dies after an initial rescue by the medical student. "The story is simple," reported *The Film Daily* (October 5, 1938), "but it gets over because of its very simplicity and charm, and the sea action and bleakness of the island and its poor inhabitants and their lives get away from the routine Hollywood production."

In an effort to assuage the thirst of Irish-Americans for native Irish productions, American distributors would often resort to subterfuge. A New York–based distributor, the Dublin Film Company, took a 1937 British feature, *Rose of Tralee*, and released it in the United States in 1938 as an Irish film. The name of the director and screenwriter—Oswald Mitchell—was conveniently forgotten and the emphasis placed on the story's being written by the Irish Kathleen Tyrone. The star, child actress Binkie Stuart, had been known in the United Kingdom as "the British Shirley Temple." The Dublin Film Company rechristened her "the Shirley Temple of Ireland." Presumably Irish-American audiences (who now had their own theatre, the Irish, formerly the Miami) were satisfied with the presence on screen, in supporting roles, of Danny Malone and Kathleen O'Regan, and the inclusion of some five "Irish" songs, "Rose of Tralee," "The Mountains of Mourne," "Down on Finnegan's Farm," "Believe Me if All Those Endearing Young Charms," and "Did Your Mother Come from Ireland."

The last "Irish" film to reach the United States prior to the Second World War was *Here Is Ireland*, a two-hour travelogue, produced, photographed and narrated by Pat Stanton. Shot in color, *Here Is Ireland* was promoted to show its audience "the improvements in your town and country." *Variety* (October 9, 1940) was not particularly impressed, commenting that much of it "could easily pass for projected picture post cards."

During the Second World War, Ireland maintained total neutrality to the extent that none of the great British wartime features could be screened there, nor could such innocuous films as 20th Century–Fox's *A Yank in the R.A.F.* (1941). The Irish never got to see the two German features—*Der Fuchs von Glenarvon/The Fox of Glenarvon* (1940) and *Mein Leben für Irland/My Life for Ireland* (1941)—directed by Max W. Kimmich at Goebbels' request, and presenting a Nazi view of Ireland's revolt against the British. The latter film is of the most interest in its depiction of an English boarding school to which the sons of Irish revolutionaries are sent to learn to be English gentlemen. They are told: "When you appreciate the profound significance of the British right to sovereignty over other nations—that is, her civilising mission—and when you act accordingly, it will be then that you will lead a free and happy life" and that "Britain's colonial policy has from the start been governed by the great Christian principle of love of one's fellowmen, even if on occasion she has used force, relentless force, this has happened only when immature peoples opposed measures which were only for their own good."

A third film, *Leinen aus Irland/Linen from Ireland* (1939) is often cited as an example of anti-British, pro-Irish propaganda, but this is not the case. It involves a Jewish businessman who attempts to destroy the weaving industry of the Sudetenland by importing duty-free Irish linen.

The Motion Picture Producers and Distributors of America was somewhat concerned with Irish neutrality, and, in 1943, sent Martin Quigley, Jr. on a five-month visit to Eire to look into the question. He reported, "The people, who are generally amply militant and articulate, are entirely in accord with anything that the government says is in behalf of the neutrality."

The neutrality of Ireland persuaded Laurence Olivier to film *Henry V* (1945) there. The Battle of Agincourt was shot at the Powerscourt estate at Enniskerry, County Wicklow, with the men of Ireland—more than 650 of them—providing cheap labor at £3.5 a week. Those who could also provide horses were paid an additional £2. Shooting commenced in Ireland on June 9 and was completed by July 22, at a cost of £80,000.

Film production revived, to a limited extent, in Ireland after the Second World War. In the spring of 1946, Eire Films, Ltd. announced the creation of a new Irish newsreel company, with capitalization of $250,000. Its first production, which does not appear to have been released in the United States, was *Mirror of Ireland*. In 1948, John H. Furbay produced and narrated an 81-minute color travelogue, *Ireland Today*. "The photography ranks at the top of the amateur or the bottom of the professional class," commented *Motion Picture Herald* (June 26, 1948). "While some Irish-Americans will be attracted by the film and entertained, it is an inadequate treatment of 'Ireland Today'."

In 1951, Hilton Edwards wrote and directed a two-reel short subject, in 35mm, for the Gate Theatre, and titled *Return to Glennascaul*. English-born Hilton Edwards (1903–1982) had co-founded the Gate Theatre, Dublin, with Micheál Mac Liammóir in 1928, at which time he also became Mac Liammóir's lover. The two were affectionately known as "Sodom and Begorrah." *Return to Glennascaul* is a ghost story, in which Mac Liammóir tells Orson Welles of accepting a ride with two ladies. He stops for a cup of tea "or something stronger" at their pleasant home, departs, but later returns to retrieve his cigarette case which he had accidentally left behind. Upon his return, he finds the house desolate, and is told by a real estate agent that the two ladies whom he met had died years earlier. However, his cigarette case is where he left it, on the mantlepiece.

Orson Welles was a long-time friend of Edwards and Mac Liammóir. He had come to the Gate Theatre in October of 1931, persuading Edwards that he was a visiting American actor and gaining employment. Initially Mac Liammóir was jealous of Edwards' friendship with the handsome young American. However, a friendship developed between the three men which was to last through their lives, with Mac Liammóir's playing Iago to Welles' Othello in the actor's 1952 screen version of the Shakespeare play.

In 1958, Irish entrepreneurs Emmet Dalton and Louis Elliman acquired

Micheál Mac Liammóir (left) with Orson Welles in *Othello*.

the site of a former riding stable and created the Ardmore Studios—the name means "high places" in Gaelic—some 12 miles outside of Dublin, near the town of Bray, County Wicklow. Covering approximately 40 acres, and with a Georgian manor house as its administrative centre, the studios boasted three sound stages and the usual editing and dubbing facilities. Ardmore Studios were, and remain, Ireland's only studio film complex.

The first film to be shot at Ardmore was *Home Is the Hero*, an adaptation of Walter Macken's play, starring Macken, along with one American, Arthur Kennedy, and various members of the Abbey Theatre company (including Eileen Crowe and Harry Brogan). Emmet Dalton had made an arrangement with RKO to produce a series of very low budget features, of which this was the first, and RKO assigned director Fielder Cook (who had no Irish connections) to the project.

Fielder Cook remembers Dalton as "a man of absolute steel and a great gentleman." He was pleased with Ardmore Studios largely because everything was brand new. Arthur Kennedy was his choice of leading man, although Kennedy's role is subordinate to Walter Macken's. Cook recalls that the Abbey Theatre players were each paid five dollars a day, regardless of the size of the role each was playing.

Although Cook was permitted an English cinematographer, Stanley Pavey, he was not allowed to bring in an outside sound crew. "I almost went back home," says Cook, remembering his problems in trying to find an adequate sound man in the Irish Republic. Even worse, Cook was not allowed to bring a "dolly man" (who operates the camera crane) into the country. No such personnel were available in the Republic, and the problem appeared insurmountable. However, one evening Macken and Cook were walking alongside the Liffey in Dublin and came to the dock area. Both of them had the same idea immediately upon seeing the cranes there. They walked around until they found a reasonably young Irish crane worker, and asked if he might be interested in entering the film industry. The worker eventually agreed, as did his union, and Ireland got its first dolly man.

Home Is the Hero is the story of Paddo O'Reilly, a man of enormous physical strength but limited mental ability who makes life miserable for his family before his son, Willy, eventually takes command. The film was released in the United Kingdom by British Lion/Britannia. *The Monthly Film Bulletin* (February 1960) found it to be "the familiar blend of melodrama, pathos and farce," but praised Fielder Cook for his "spirited direction," which "avoids visual monotony and goes all out for the big scenes." *Variety* (March 11, 1959) commented, "Director Fielder Cook has caught atmosphere of group, and the settings are effective. This seems to rate top billing as a piece which is Irish."

By the time *Home Is the Hero* was released in the United States—in 1961—RKO had ceased to exist as a distribution entity, and the film was handled by Show Corp. of America. In *Cue* (January 28, 1961), Jesse Zunser wrote that Macken's play "in film form . . . has been broadened, deepened, tightened and enriched by solidly integrated Abbey Theatre performances. . . . It's a typically Irish drama, written in lilting musical fashion." *Newsweek* (February 6, 1961) described *Home Is the Hero* as "a moving and beautifully acted story about the complexities of 'simple' people."

Following *Home Is the Hero*, the first major production to be shot at Ardmore was *Shake Hands with the Devil*, filmed in 1959, directed by Michael Anderson, and starring James Cagney, Don Murray, Dana Wynter, Glynis Johns, Michael Redgrave, and Sybil Thorndike, supported by a group of Irish players, including Cyril Cusack, Eileen Crowe, Niall MacGinnis, and Noel Purcell.

Ardmore Studios was never to be a financially successful operation, and in 1962, it went into receivership. The complex was sold in 1967 to the New

Kevin McClory (left) and Richard Harris with John Lavery's portrait of Michael Collins; the film *Michael Collins* was to have been produced at Ardmore Studios early in 1969.

Brighton Tower Company, but again entered receivership, and in 1973 was purchased for a reported $800,000 by the Irish government through Radio Telefís Éireann, on behalf of the Minister for Industry and Commerce. Renamed the National Film Studios in 1975, the complex came under the nominal control of producer/director John Boorman, who was named its unpaid chairman, and who was actively involved in major film production in the Republic.

The Irish government closed the facility in 1982, at which time Boorman resigned, and there was an outpouring of protest from the likes of Princess Grace of Monaco, Peter Ustinov, King Vidor, Jack Valenti, and John Huston. Boorman's chairmanship had been criticized by some Irish film commentators, such as Kevin Rockett, while the Association of Independent Producers of Ireland (later called the Association of Independent Film-makers) had fought Boorman as an outsider — an Englishman — who had tried to gain control of the financing of Irish film production, and yet Boorman was, to a certain extent, the last major figure involved in Irish cinema, and almost its last hope for a rosy future. In 1984, Ardmore was purchased by the Pakistani shipping magnate Mahmoud Sipra for $1,000,000. A year later, it changed hands again when the American-based MTM Enterprises gained permission from the Irish courts to acquire the property.

The history of Ardmore Studios is as checkered as that of Irish government support, or lack of it, for film production. It was not until 1982 that an Irish Film Board (Bord Scannán n hÉireann or BSÉ) was created. It has made investments and loans to Irish-based films, and urges tax incentives from the government (usually without much success).

Two other important Emmet Dalton productions were *Broth of a Boy* (1959) and *The Poacher's Daughter* (1960). The former, directed by George Pollock, starred Barry Fitzgerald as a 110-year-old man, with Harry Brogan as his 80-year-old son. Based on the play *The Big Birthday* (the original Irish release title) by Hugh Leonard, the film provided plenty of comic opportunities for Fitzgerald. *The Poacher's Daughter*, released in Ireland as *Sally's Irish Rogue*, was based on a play, *The New Gossoon*, by George Shiels, which had first been seen on the New York stage in 1930. Directed by George Pollock, and starring Julie Harris in the title role and supported by members of the Abbey Theatre Company, the film was reasonably successful on its American release, generally playing on a double bill with the British comedy *Carry On Admiral*. Typical of the critical reaction was that of John McCarten (who eventually retired to Dublin) in the *New Yorker* (March 5, 1960): "While the content of *The Poacher's Daughter* is slight, the dialogue is diverting, and the cast assuredly knows how to line it out."

Other Emmet Dalton productions from Ardmore include *This Other Eden* (1959), directed by Muriel Box and starring Audrey Dalton, Leslie Phillips and Niall McGinnis; *Lies My Father Told Me*, directed by Don Chaffey, and featuring Harry Brogan and Betsy Blair; and *The Devil's Agent*, directed by John Paddy Carstairs, and starring Peter Van Eyck, Macdonald Carey and Christopher Lee.

The most important feature to be produced at Ardmore at this time was *The Quare Fellow*, based on the Brendan Behan play, and directed by Arthur Dreifuss for British Lion–Bryanston. The film, which was released in the United States in 1963, featured Sylvia Sims, Patrick McGoohan, Walter Macken, Harry Brogan, and Hilton Edwards. Bosley Crowther, writing in the *New York Times* (February 20, 1963) felt that the production had "a harsh Irish eloquence about it and a certain brutal dramatic punch." *Time* (March 8, 1963) called the film "a funny tragedy, a happy-go-lucky horror show, a gay little wake for the dead who have died in the name of justice — the kind of justice that demands a life for a life. Like the play, the picture ignores the rational arguments against capital punishment. It simply takes its audience inside an Irish prison and bolts the gate; and then with a world of Irish charm and humor shows everybody how it feels to live in a cell — and die on a rope."

Writing in *The New Republic* (March 30, 1963), Stanley Kauffmann, after viewing *The Quare Fellow, Home Is the Hero* and *The Playboy of the Western World*, opined that "The Irish film, in any large consequential sense, does not yet exist. What is needed perhaps is a transmutation of the Irish poetic sense from flow of word to flow of vision; the dramatic sense is already there in abundance. If the new medium ever truly touches Irish fancy and anger, the small country may have as disproportionately large an effect on films as it has had on other arts."

When *The Quare Fellow* first opened in New York, the city was suffering from a newspaper strike which prevented the film's receiving much publicity. As a result, it was reissued in 1966 to further enthusiastic reviews. In 1960, Louis Elliman produced a film at Ardmore, *Meet the Quare Fellow*, featuring Brendan Behan and well-known Irish television personality Eamonn Andrews.

In 1965, Charles Davis directed a 90-minute documentary on President John F. Kennedy's 1963 visit to the Republic of Ireland, released as *Kennedy's Ireland*. While many Americans might perceive of that film, with its travelogue and patronizing approach, as typical of Irish documentary filmmaking, in reality the country has a fine tradition in the field dating back to the late thirties, when the Irish Film Society started a film school, graduates of which include George Morrison, Patrick Carey, Brendan Stafford, and Colm O'Leary.

The establishment of the television service of RTÉ (Radio Telefís Éireann) in 1961 — the radio service began in January 1926 — provided regular employment for many Irish filmmakers. In 1959, the Reverend Joseph Dunne founded the "Radharc" Film Unit to produce religious programs for RTÉ, and in February 1967 opened a Communications Centre in Dublin. Gael-Linn has sponsored many documentaries, but deliberately limits its audience by refusing to permit its Gaelic films to be dubbed into English. Thus, non–Gaelic speaking audiences have been denied access to George Morrison's fine series of documentaries on twentieth century Irish history, beginning with *Mise Éire* (1959) and *Saoirse?* (1961).

Among the best of the contemporary documentary filmmakers are Patrick Carey, Kieran Hickey and Louis Marcus. The last has received two Academy Award nominations for his short subjects, *Children at Work* (1973) and *Conquest of Light* (1975). In 1978, Marcus produced a series of six hour-long documentaries on *The Heritage of Ireland*. Dublin-born Patrick Carey has also received Oscar nominations for *Yeats Country* (1965) and *Oisin* (1970). His films are rightly noted for their pictorial beauty. He believes that the future of film lies in the short subject, and, back in 1970, he told the author, "Film is highly developed as a narrative art and can keep pace with modern literature, but as a plastic art, like music, painting or sculpture, it is far, far behind the modern movement. With rare exceptions it is simply waffling around looking for somewhere to go."

Two Irish filmmakers in exile have produced very divergent documentary films on their homeland. Peter Lennon, a journalist living in Paris, was responsible for *Rocky Road to Dublin* (1968), a feature-length examination of what has happened to his country since 1916. According to Lennon, "Americans always think—especially vulgar Americans—that Ireland is funny because the Irish drink so much and clown so much for visitors. They have imagination, you see, and no way of using it." *Rocky Road to Dublin* is, Lennon claims, "a personal description of a community which survived nearly 700 years of English occupation and then nearly sank under the weight of its own heroes and clergy."[12] He attacks the Church and the middle classes, arguing that the revolution is far from over in the Republic, and, as if to emphasize his viewpoint, Lennon utilizes Raoul Coutard, a favorite of revolutionary filmmaker Jean Luc Godard, as his cinematographer.

An equally personal, and far more subdued view of Ireland is given by BBC editor Colin Hill in his 1971 documentary short, *Dark Moon Hollow*, which tells of an old man's pilgrimage along the River Lee, from Cork Harbor to its source at Gougane Barra, near the shrine of St. Finbarr (the founder of Cork).

In 1972, French filmmaker Marcel Ophuls came to Ireland to film a documentary on the turmoil in Northern Ireland, very much in the manner of his highly successful, if overlong, *The Sorrow and the Pity*. The resultant film, *A Sense of Loss*, was a two-hour and thirteen-minute biased view of Northern Ireland, which was heavily slanted towards the Catholic minority (although one of the participants, Bernadette Devlin, hardly did her cause much good). Ophuls claimed that his film was intended to make the politics of Northern Ireland understandable. In reality, *A Sense of Loss* further confuses an already confused, and tragic, issue, and fails to suggest any solution—apart from that offered by one of the interviewees, that all the churches and priests of Ireland be taken on a raft out into the Atlantic Ocean and sunk. *A Sense of Loss* did, however, indicate what was to be the source of inspiration for much native film production that was to follow, and that was Northern Ireland.

Of course, Northern Ireland had already been featured in at least two earlier British films. Carol Reed's *Odd Man Out* (1947) presented a moving, humanistic drama of a rebel leader on the run through the Belfast streets, with fine performances by James Mason, Robert Newton, Kathleen Ryan, F.J. McCormick, and Fay Compton. *A Terrible Beauty* (1960), filmed at Ardmore Studios and directed by the American Tay Garnett, featured Robert Mitchum, Anne Heywood, Cyril Cusack, and Richard Harris and is a dreary drama involving the Nazis' supplying arms to IRA terrorists in Ulster. But these were decidedly British views of the IRA and Northern Ireland, and now a new breed of young Irish filmmakers was ready to present its side of the story.

Funded largely by the British Film Institute, *Maeve* (1981) is concerned with a young Irish woman (played by Mary Jackson) who returns to Northern Ireland to visit her family in Belfast, after a number of years in London. First screened at the Cork Film Festival in 1981, *Maeve* was directed by Pat Murphy, who was born in Dublin but had lived as a teenager in Belfast. Ms. Murphy is also responsible for *Anne Devlin* (1984), largely financed by the Irish Film

Board, which is the story of an Irish patriot who helped Robert Emmet in his unsuccessful revolt against the British in the early nineteenth century. Brid Brennan, who had also appeared in *Maeve*, has the title role.

Produced at a cost of approximately £500,000, *Anne Devlin* was filmed on location at Strokestown House, County Roscommon, some 80 miles from Dublin, and was promoted—somewhat incorrectly—as the first feature to be financed, cast and crewed entirely in Ireland. American response to the film— it was first seen at the Los Angeles International Film Festival (Filmex) on July 8, 1984—was somewhat subdued. *Daily Variety* (July 10, 1984) commented, "Opening reels are decidedly on the slow side, and Murphy's plain, even-keeled, long-take style has both pros and cons, sacrificing in dynamism and excitement what it gains in clarity and thoroughness. Film picks up in purposefulness in the climactic sections, with Devlin's absolute refusal to cooperate with her English captors or to confess even her own obvious involvement in the rebellion emerging as both the most personally absolute and politically radical act witnessed in the entire picture."

Angel (1982) marked the directorial and screenwriting debut of Neil Jordan. It cost $1,000,000 to produce and was funded largely by the independent British commercial television organization, Channel 4, with additional funding coming from the Irish Film Board. The film was produced by Motion Picture Company of Ireland, which had been established by John Boorman, following his departure as chairman of the National Film Studios.

Set in Northern Ireland but filmed in the Republic, *Angel* is concerned with a saxophone player (Stephen Rea)—described by his band's singer as "The Stan Getz of Armagh"—who witnesses the murder of the band's manager and a deaf-mute girl witness. He becomes obsessed in tracking down the murderers, along the way becoming a murderer himself.

The film opened in Chicago in March 1985, retitled *Danny Boy*. Writing in *The Chicago Tribune* (March 15, 1985), Larry Kart commented,

> Tossing in references to the work of Michelangelo Antonioni and Ingmar Bergman, Jordan creates the feeling that Danny [the saxophone player] is a pawn in some elaborate game—a man who has like the hero of Antonioni's *Blow Up*, stumbled into one of those zones of strangeness that underlie the normal world.
>
> If that makes *Danny Boy* sound arty and pretentious, it is to some extent. But Jordan takes those gestures toward the cinematic avant-garde of the 1960s and puts them to good use, for within the context of Northern Ireland's bloodbath, such "art for art's sake" touches become an ironic cry for freedom—an insistence that, despite all the evidence to the contrary, there once was another way out.

The New York critics were bothered by the film's failure to come to grips with its subject matter. J. Hoberman in *The Village Voice* (May 29, 1984) called it "doggedly theological." In the *New York Times* (May 18, 1984), Janet Maslin noted that "*Danny Boy* displays the technical proficiency of its director,

John Lynch in *Cal*.

Neil Jordan, without making more than a fleeting claim on the audience's attention. That may make it sound like an overstylish effort, but in fact, Mr. Jordan's film has a homespun style and story, which makes its remoteness doubly odd."

The most important of the new Irish films dealing with Northern Ireland is *Cal*. It was filmed by David Puttnam's Enigma Company, with the minimum of publicity, in the Republic of Ireland, during an eight week period in the town of Drogheda. Concerned with the question of what it means to be young and Catholic in Northern Ireland, *Cal* opens with the murder of a Protestant policeman. Cal, an unemployed 19-year-old, who was once employed in a slaughterhouse, is recruited into the IRA, and gradually comes to have a romance with the policeman's widow.

The film is based on a 1983 novel by Bernard Mac Laverty, who adapted his book for the screen, and directed by Pat O'Connor, who came to producer Puttnam's attention with his study of a group of people at an Irish dance hall, *The Ballroom of Romance*, made for the BBC in 1982. (O'Connor had also directed a number of documentaries, as well as *One of Ourselves*, a 1983 BBC production about one day in the life of an Irish teenager in the fifties.) O'Connor cast Helen Mirren as the widow, and John Lynch, a Northern Ireland Catholic, making his screen debut, as Cal.

Ireland's official entry at the 1984 Cannes Film Festival, *Cal* was well received by the press both in Europe and the United States. "Politics might determine one's reaction to *Cal*," wrote Tom O'Brien in *Commonweal* (October 5, 1984). "An enthusiastic supporter of the IRA provisionals, or at least British withdrawal, would be sure to find much to criticize in its resolutely even-handed approach.... A Protestant sympathetically tells Cal after his house is burned, 'There are bad bastards on both sides.' The film ... seems to condone this sad view and provide no easy answers." In *Time* (September 3, 1984), Richard Schickel called *Cal* "a brooding, subtle film that dares to make the only valid response to the endless violence of life in Northern Ireland today: a sort of strangled horror." Janet Maslin called it "a beautiful, mournful movie" in the *New York Times* (August 24, 1984).

Interestingly, *Cal* was seen in the United States the same year that NBC aired a documentary, *Crossfire*, on the tragedy of Northern Ireland's children. It showed the work of the Children's Committee 10, and co-producer Frank Prendergast explained, "We set out to make a story about the committee. What we *damn* well don't want it to be is a perpetuation of the problem, of the cliches and mindlessness that goes on. I want the American public for two hours to come into the Northern Ireland experience and to get *past* the cliches of petrol bombs, ski-masks, British troops ... all those buzz-words that we apply to the situation."[13]

The most bloodthirsty and violent of films to deal with Northern Ireland is surely *A Quiet Day in Belfast*, a 1974 Canadian feature, produced and directed by Milad Bessada, and starring Margot Kidder and Barry Foster. The former plays twin sisters—as she had already done in Brian De Palma's *Sisters*—one of whom arrives from Canada to stay with her twin in Belfast, is mistaken for the other (having an affair with a British policeman), and shot by a sniper. Shot on location in Toronto and Dublin, *A Quiet Day in Belfast* was based on a play by Andrew Angus Dalrymple, first staged at the Tarragon Theatre in Toronto. The film bears a striking resemblance to the novel *Blood Sisters* by Valerie Miner.

As British producer Kenith Trodd has pointed out, films about Northern Ireland have suddenly become fashionable. He also notes that "it's difficult to have a rounded view because the situation is an *extremely* complicated one. The more authentic and detailed you get, the more inscrutable it becomes to the outsiders."[14] One thing remains clear, however, and that is that films dealing with Northern Ireland cannot be shot there—they must be made in Dublin—because film crews are frightened to work in the province and insurance rates are too high.

Northern Ireland is not the only topic to interest contemporary Irish filmmakers. Just as the state has become less repressive in recent years, so filmmakers have been able to tackle current isssues and problems. In 1978, Kieran Hickey directed *Exposure*, written by himself and Philip Davison, which dealt with male sexual repression and male bonding in Irish society.

Poitin/Poteen (1979) was billed as the first feature-length film to be produced in Gaelic. Director Bob Quinn argued that his film countered the image of Ireland presented by John Ford and others in films such as *The Quiet Man*. A brutal and at times unpleasant film, *Poitin* starred Cyril Cusack as a moonshiner, producing the illegal brew of poitin on the coast of Connemara. "As might be expected, the film fails to match the awesome challenge of *The Quiet Man*," commented *Daily Variety* (March 16, 1979) at its American premiere as part of Filmex on March 17, 1979, "but it does offer a contrasting, considerably more bitter view of the impoverished society in the wilds of Western Ireland."

Two major films emerged from Ireland in 1984. *Pigs* took a singularly unromantic look at Dublin life in general and, in particular, a group of squatters living in an abandoned house in the inner city. It was directed by Cathal Black, who had been responsible for *Our Boys*, a controversial documentary on the influence of the Christian Brothers teaching order in the Republic. Produced for less than £200,000 *Pig* was written by and starred Jimmy Brennan, whose character, also called Jimmy, was both a former prison inmate and a homosexual.

The Company of Wolves was Neil Jordan's first film since *Angel*. A fairy tale involving wolves, the feature starred Angela Lansbury, David Warner and Graham Crowden. Jordan wrote the screenplay with Angela Carter, from whose short story the film was adapted. Described by Vincent Canby in the *New York Times* (April 19, 1985) as a "movie that looks like a cross between something from Jean Cocteau, not at peak form, and a horror movie from Hammer," it is basically the story of Little Red Riding Hood, told with explicit detail, finding the darker, more horrific aspects within the classic fairy tale.

There is a new breed of filmmaker very much alive and well in the Republic of Ireland. He (and she) owes nothing to the Ireland of John Ford or Celtic romanticism. The contemporary Irish filmmaker presents an image of the country that is both realistic and honest. The myth has been forgotten. The reality is all that matters.

II. The American Film Producer in Ireland

The influence of the American film producer in Ireland has been both far-reaching and positive, with his presence affecting the country both economically and politically. The American film producer was there at the beginning of the Irish film industry—if "industry" it may be called. His presence was felt immediately prior to the 1916 Easter Rebellion. And it was an American who influenced the Irish government in the proposed, and as it proved abortive, establishment of a national film industry.

Ireland has, of course, always held a fascination for Americans, be they of Irish descent or not. Its romantic image has appealed to many in the film industry, whose links to the country were either nebulous or nonexistent. The Italian-born Rudolph Valentino, who became the screen's first legendary star thanks to his performances in *The Four Horsemen of the Apocalypse* and *The Sheik* and, above all, to his premature death in 1926, felt the attraction of Ireland. In a 1923 book of verse, *Daydreams*,[1] is one titled "Erin":

> The green sod is red now—
> Rebellion.
> The green sod is white now—
> Purity.
> The green sod is blue now,
> with truth.
> And the green sod is ever green.
> It is growth—none can stop natural growth.
> Erin—land of dreams—Awaken.

Great poetry it may not be, but the sentiment is honest enough. At the height of his fame, Valentino was a Paramount star, and it was the heads of that studio—Adolph Zukor and Jesse L. Lasky—who sent an American film crew (including director Victor Heerman and stars Lois Wilson and Thomas Meighan) over to Ireland in 1925 to film a romantic feature titled *Irish Luck*. Here the sentiment is far easier to understand. It was strictly a commercial proposition. *Irish Luck* was a film designed to appeal to the multitude of Irish immigrants who comprised a sizeable percentage of the filmgoing audience during the cinema's silent years.

Ireland also responded to the presence of these screen personalities. Thomas Meighan was invited to meet President William Cosgrave; he went to kiss the Blarney Stone — an episode incorporated into the feature — and John McCormack took the actor on a tour of the countryside around Dublin.

The star of *Irish Luck*, Thomas Meighan, was a favorite of Adolph Zukor, who crossed over the Atlantic with his star on the *Leviathan*, and hosted a formal dinner aboard the ship on July 30, 1925. (Also present at the dinner were Mrs. Meighan, Charlotte Greenwood, Martin Broones, Victor Heerman, Thomas Geraghty, Lou Sarecky, and Emmet Crozier.)

From Ireland, Meighan reported back to Lasky and Zukor — in a letter dated August 12, 1925, from the Shelbourne Hotel, Dublin:

> We arrived here in Dublin last Friday after-noon and got a marvelous reception, thousands and thousands of people to greet us both when we got off the boat and at the hotel. We got our race track scenes Saturday and finished here to-day. We are leaving for Killarney early in the morning, arrive there at two in the after-noon. We are breaking our necks to catch the Leviathan Aug. 25th. The people here have been wonderful to us except on one or two occasions the crowds on the streets were so enormous we could not work, we had to stop and go back to the location again. John McCormack and Mac-Sweeney are here and helped a great deal in many ways. Sunday we had tea with the President of Ireland. We feel we are going to have a fine picture and with some very interesting and colorful scenes of Ireland. I am on the water [wagon] and this is a tough country to be in and not take a drink.

It was a knowledge of the Irish dominance in the make-up of early theatre audiences that must have influenced the New York–based Kalem Company to send a group of filmmakers to Ireland in the summer of 1910. In many ways, the decision by Kalem's president, Frank Marion, was a revolutionary one. Not only was he sending the first American filmmakers to Ireland, but he was also endorsing the idea of shooting on foreign locations — a concept which was to lead to Kalem's producing the five-reel feature *From the Manger to the Cross* in Palestine in the spring of 1912, and the Vitagraph Company's sending a party, headed by its leading man, Maurice Costello, on a six-month trip around the world, beginning in December 1912.

The Kalem group, which came to Ireland in August 1910, consisted of actress/screenwriter Gene Gauntier, actor Robert Vignola, cinematographer George K. Hollister, and director Sidney Olcott. The last was of Irish descent, and, according to his leading lady, "possessed all the sparkle and sentiment of that emotional people." They landed at what was then Queenstown (and is now Cobh), briefly visited Cork, and then moved on to Killarney in search of a suitable location to set up an open-air studio. That they found in the village of Beaufort, some eight miles outside of Killarney, a picturesque community

Members of the Kalem Company gathered outside Patrick O'Sullivan's home in Beaufort, County Kerry.

nestled under the shadow of the McGillicuddy Reeks, and one which looks today much as it did 65 years ago. The group took up residence in the home of Patrick O'Sullivan, building a wooden platform in the field behind the house, which was to serve as the company's studio. Here was filmed Ireland's first fictional film, a one-reel short titled *The Lad from Old Ireland*, released in the United States on November 23, 1910. The group also shot footage of Irish landmarks such as Blarney Castle, as well as a second one-reel short, *The Irish Honeymoon*.

The Kalem Company returned to Ireland again in the summers of 1911 and 1912 with a considerably expanded company, which now included Gene Gauntier's husband, Jack Clark, actress and wardrobe mistress Agnes Mapes, actress Alice Hollister (the wife of cinematographer George), actor J.P. McGowan, actor Robert Vignola, and set designer and constructor Allen Farnham. The village of Beaufort became not merely the filmmaking capital of Ireland, it was the only area of filmmaking in the country.

Relationships between the villagers and the American filmmakers were good, marred only by one incident in 1911, when the local parish priest attacked the Americans as "tramp photographers," whose films were intended

Jack Clark is hiding under Gene Gauntier's cloak in *Rory O'More*.

"to degrade the Irish." The local bishop and the American consul in Queenstown came to the assistance of the filmmakers, and the priest apologized for his remarks. The group also appears to have enjoyed a satisfactory relationship with the British authorities. No effort was made to hamper or interfere with the work of the O'Kalem's—as they were now, jokingly, referred to—despite the pro-nationalistic, anti–British slant of many of their films. Among such subjects were *Rory O'More* (1911), *The O'Neill* (1912) and *Ireland the Oppressed* (1912).

When not dealing with Irish nationalism in their films, the O'Kalems were shooting one-reel shorts which showed the natural beauties of Ireland, and screen versions of popular "Irish" dramas such as Joseph Murphy's *The Kerry Gow* and *Shaun Rhue* (both released in 1912), and Dion Boucicault's *The Colleen Bawn* (also filmed by the Yankee Film Company in the United States in 1911) and *Arrah-na-Pogue*, both released in 1911. Joseph Murphy's plays had been touring in the United States for more than 30 years prior to their filming, and Murphy was able to advise the company on their production.

There is no question as to the popularity of these Kalem Irish films in the United States. As late as 1914, Kalem reissued *The Colleen Bawn*, and in connection therewith devised a novel publicity stunt involving the shipment to New York of several tons of soil from the base of the Colleen Bawn Rock. This soil was portioned into trays, which were distributed with the film, and patrons were encouraged, prior to the film's screening, to stand—literally—on Irish soil! Following the 1916 Easter Rebellion, Kalem reissued *The O'Neill*—a drama of a patriot who takes to highway robbery to raise funds for the cause of Irish freedom—under the title of *The Irish Rebel*.

When Sidney Olcott and Gene Gauntier quit the Kalem Company in the fall of 1912, they formed their own company and returned to Beaufort in the summer of 1913 to film *For Ireland's Sake* and *Come Back to Erin*. Again, in the summer of 1914, Sidney Olcott returned to Beaufort, this time with his actress wife, Valentine Grant, to film *The Irish in America* and *Bold Emmett, Ireland's Martyr*. Had it not been for the First World War, it is highly probable that Olcott would have continued to spend his summers filming in Beaufort, and it is equally possible that the village might one day have boasted a permanent studio facility.

The summer of 1912 also saw the visit to Ireland by a small group of filmmakers from the Brooklyn-based Vitagraph Company, headed by jovial and rotund comedian John Bunny and director Larry Trimble. Vitagraph filmed two one-reel comedies in Ireland: *Michael McShane, Matchmaker* and *The Blarney Stone*. In the former, released in the United States on November 6, 1912, Bunny, in the title role, helps Dan O'Toole (played by Charles Cox) win the hand of Colleen O'Brien (played by Mabelle Lumley). *The Blarney Stone*, released in the United States on March 28, 1913, cast Bunny as an Englishman, named, of all things, John Bull. While taking his daughter, played by Mabelle Lumley, on a trip to Ireland, Bunny is persuaded to kiss the Blarney Stone, with the result that he discovers he is so happy that he can consent to his daughter's marriage to her lover, played by George Cox. Larry Trimble also filmed two half-reel travelogue subjects in Ireland: *Scenes of Irish Life in Dublin*, released October 23, 1912, and *Cork and Vicinity*, released on December 6, 1912. John Bunny took time out to visit the Rotunda Theatre in Dublin, where he praised its Irish Ladies Orchestra, commenting, "An orchestra composed of women is an undeniable asset to every hall in the world."

From a political viewpoint, the most influential American to visit Ireland during the silent era was Walter Macnamara. Born in County Waterford in 1876, Macnamara had been educated in Wales and came to the United States as a young man, enjoying a career as a war correspondent in South Africa, a novelist, comedian, and actor. According to *The Moving Picture World* (November 8, 1913), he was also one of the first vice presidents of the Gaelic League and one of the founders of the Irish Club in London. Under contract to Universal, Macnamara wrote a tawdry screen melodrama, *Traffic in Souls*, released in 1913, which dealt with the then-popular subject of "white slavery."

The nature of this film gives a fairly clear indication of Macnamara's character. He was an opportunist. In January 1914, he formed his own company, and, a month later, sailed for London, where he began filming — at the Ec-ko Studios at Kew Bridge — a political feature titled *Ireland a Nation*. The film was intended as a complete history of Ireland from 1798 through 1914. Exteriors were filmed in Ireland by Macnamara, who was arrested on arrival for importing arms into the country, arms which he insisted were merely "props" to be used in his production. Between filming in Ireland, Macnamara rallied citizens to the nationalist cause.

In an interview with George Blaisdell of *The Moving Picture World*, Walter Macnamara discussed the filming:

> Did I have any difficulties in finding locations? Yes, in one instance, certainly, when I tried to find a mud hut and failed. Parnell wiped those out. I did, though, get some wonderful backgrounds, as I think you will agree when you see the picture. Here is a fort built by Oliver Cromwell. To this day no real son of the old sod passes it without spitting — that's the only way he can adequately express his feelings for the builder. I have tried to get absolute accuracy in my backgrounds — authentic locations — and I think I have succeeded.
>
> Were any obstacles placed in my path in the making of *Ireland a Nation*? Yes, indeed, by the soldiers. Sometimes we would start to take a scene with not a soul in sight. It seemed sometimes that in two minutes soldiers would come from everywhere and demand to see a permit. Think of having a permit to take the side of a mountain! Of course, the picture was revolutionary in character, and the military tried in every way to handicap us. That's why we were five months over there. The people? They couldn't do enough for us. The Nationalist Party gave us unofficial sanction.[2]

Ireland a Nation received its world premiere at New York's 44th Street Theatre on September 22, 1914. The critics were not terribly impressed. *Variety* noted, "The producer has overlooked scores of opportunities to make the picture effective. The whole is not too well produced and the acting cast, numbering sixteen, discloses but one capable actor in the person of Barney Magee."[3] *The Moving Picture World* commented, "The production covers a vast amount of ground for a five-reel subject, and if it is to be criticized for anything it is the constant shifting of the interest from one character to another."[4] The critics notwithstanding, *Ireland a Nation* proved tremendously popular with Irish-American audiences and helped raise both moral and financial support for the cause of Irish independence.

The film's Irish premiere was somewhat delayed because the first prints shipped from New York to Europe were on board the *Lusitania*, which was sunk by a German submarine off the Irish coast on May 7, 1915. It is more than a little ironic that while Irish nationalists supported Germany during the First World War, it was a German torpedo which prevented Ireland from seeing a film aimed at promoting the Irish nationalist cause.

Ireland a Nation eventually opened in Dublin, at the Rotunda, on January 8, 1917, less than six months after the execution of the sixteenth leader of the Easter Week Rising, one of whom, incidentally, Michael Mallin, ran a cinema on Dublin's New Street. Joseph Holloway, the noted observer of the Dublin theatre scene, wrote, "Truly the man who thought of the title *Ireland a Nation* was worth his weight in gold to the film company that produced it. It is the title and not the film drama which will attract all patriotic Dublin to the Rotunda during the week." However, it was both the title and the drama which disturbed the military authorities. On January 10, the management of the Rotunda was ordered to cease screening the film, despite its being approved for exhibition by both the British Board of Film Censors and the Military Censor of Dublin. The reason given for its suppression was that audiences cheered at the film's suggestion that "England's difficulty was Ireland's opportunity," and at the murder of an English soldier by an Irish rebel. Holloway wrote, "The film was largely booked for the provinces but the suppression cancels all these arrangements.... Anything Irish is loathsome to the military and must be stamped out of the people's pleasures here in Ireland.... In O'Connell Street a man was pasting green sheets of paper on the announcement on hoarding of *Ireland a Nation*. Only a field of green would soon show where *Ireland a Nation* once proclaimed itself."

Ireland a Nation reappeared in 1920, when the *New York Dramatic Mirror* (November 6, 1920) reported that the film was playing at the Valencia Theatre in San Francisco. "This picture is said to have been smuggled out of Ireland after the cast was jailed by Scotland Yard detectives," reported the paper, quite erroneously. That 1920 reissue print included newsreel footage of Eamon De Valera. Its distributor was the Gaelic Amusement Company, which also released, in 1920, two short subjects titled *Financing the Irish Republic* and *Forty-Five Minutes in Ireland*. Long considered a "lost" film, the 1920 version was discovered by me some 13 years ago, when the author was associate archivist of the American Film Institute, and *Ireland a Nation* is now preserved in the National Film Collection at the Library of Congress.

The First World War, together with the continuing "troubles" in Ireland, effectively ended the visits of American film producers for the remainder of the years of silent filmmaking. Travelogues and interest shorts concerning Ireland continued to be produced, of course, items such as the Burton Holmes–Paramount release, *In Old Ireland*, first seen by American audiences on October 9, 1916. Burton Holmes was also responsible for a 1930 short, *Dublin and Nearby*, released by M-G-M, in which Holmes assured his viewers that:

> The traveler will find that Ireland is one of the richest countries in the world. Rich in many things richer nations lack. Ireland is rich in beauty, in courtesy, in romance, in patriotism, and very rich in faith, and now at last Ireland is rich in liberty. Dublin has again taken her place amongst the capital cities of the older world. As the Metropolis of the Irish Free State, Dublin is a city every traveler should know.

While Burton Holmes was introducing filmgoers to Dublin, his rival film partner, James Fitzpatrick, was promoting *Ireland, the Melody Isle*, which Broadway filmgoers first saw on March 12, 1932.

Even Will Rogers was filmed visiting Irish tourist spots. Carl Stearns Clancy featured him in two 1927 short subjects, *With Will Rogers in Dublin* and *Roaming the Emerald Isle with Will Rogers*. It seems more than probable that the Rogers films were made when the comedian was in Ireland to appear in a benefit performance for the victims of a fire, on September 5, 1926, at a theatre in Drumcollogher, County Limerick, in which 48 persons died, during a screening of Cecil B. De Mille's *The Ten Commandments*.

One major American production which dates from the troubled period in Irish history is *Ireland in Revolt*, photographed by Captain Edwin F. Weigle with titles by his wife, for the *Chicago Tribune*, and released by the American Film Company in February 1921. Weigle had been a member of the U.S. Signal Corps and photographed many events in Europe during the First World War. In six reels of film, Captain Weigle depicted the ruins, mobs, barbed wire, and machine guns of Ireland in the 1920–1921 period, comparing it to the tranquility of the Irish scene in the 'teens years. According to contemporary press reports, the documentary was remarkably nonpartisan in showing barbarous tactics used by both the Sinn Feiners and the Royal Irish Constabulary. It showed the arrest, by the Black and Tans, of a Nationalist prisoner in Belfast, together with the funeral of martyred Cork mayor Terrence McSwiney.

"The picture cannot offend Irish opinion in any particular and ought to be a sensational money maker in districts where there is a large population of Celtic origin," reported *Variety* (January 14, 1921). "As a business proposition, the film has all the marks of a winner. It should attract the interest of the Irish societies, a powerful element in its favor."

The first American sound feature to utilize Irish footage was *Song o' My Heart*, directed in 1930 by Frank Borzage for the William Fox Company, and featuring John McCormack and, making her screen debut, a young nonprofessional actress from County Roscommon, Maureen O'Sullivan. Legend has it that Miss O'Sullivan was discovered by the film crew while the company was shooting location scenes at McCormack's home in Monasterevan, County Kildare.

Song o' My Heart, while it is supposedly loosely—very loosely—based on McCormack's life, is a somewhat dull and plodding production, of interest today chiefly because it records on film McCormack performing no less than 11 songs—"Then You'll Remember Me," "A Fairy Story by the Fire," "Just for Today," "I Feel You Near Me," "Kitty, My Love," "The Rose of Tralee," "Loughi Sereni e Cari," "Little Boy Blue," "Ireland, Mother Ireland," "I Hear You Calling Me," and "A Pair of Blue Eyes"—accompanied on the piano by his longtime associate on the concert platform, Edwin Schneider. There is something quaintly charming in the manner in which McCormack continually looks down at his little book of lyrics, as if he cannot remember the words for

John McCormack (left), Maureen O'Sullivan and John Garrick in *Song o' My Heart*.

songs he must have long ago committed to memory. The scenes of McCormack singing were not filmed in Ireland, but at a concert presented at the Los Angeles Philharmonic Auditorium.

Although the film and its players, including Alice Joyce, Tommy Clifford (another Irish discovery), John Garrick, J.M. Kerrigan, and J. Farrell Mac-Donald, failed to evoke much excitement from contemporary reviewers, all were full of praise for McCormack. "But who cares about the other actors or the story or anything else," commented *Photoplay*, "when there stands McCormack right before your very eyes, singing with all the tenderness and beauty for which his voice is famed? You will find yourself reaching for the dry handkerchief. See it by all means."[5]

If John McCormack was the major figure in *Song o' My Heart*, the same is not true of *Wings of the Morning*, which was shot in part on location in Ireland in 1936 and is historically important as the first *British* Technicolor feature. Although technically a British production, *Wings of the Morning* was directed by an American, Harold Schuster, starred an American leading man, Henry Fonda, and a French leading lady, Annabella, and was produced by an American, Robert T. Kane, for his New World Pictures (which appears to have been financed by 20th Century-Fox).

Wings of the Morning lacks narrative appeal and entertains today only

Maggie Dirrane, the "leading lady" in Robert Flaherty's *Man of Aran*.

with the beauty of its Technicolor photography. Although set primarily in Ireland, the bulk of the film was shot at the Denham Studios, just outside of London, with the second unit director having spent two weeks shooting location scenes in the Irish Republic. The last sequence in the film to be shot, obviously as an afterthought, is of John McCormack singing three songs. Although McCormack's appearance brings the film to a grinding halt, it does provide an opportunity for some exquisite glimpses of Irish scenery which a blind Irish aristocrat, played by Helen Haye (not the American star), visualizes as McCormack sings "Killarney."

The film opened in the United States at Radio City Music Hall on March 11, 1937, and was well liked by the critics and the public. Both seemed to agree that one word summed up the production: "Charming."

American documentary filmmaker Robert Flaherty came to Ireland in 1932 to commence work on a feature-length study of life on the Aran Islands, off the west coast of the Republic. The finished film, *Man of Aran*, released in the United States in 1934, depicts life on the islands as it must have been 100 years ago but possibly not as it was in 1932. In 1977, George Stoney produced a second documentary, *How the Myth Was Made*, which examines Flaherty's filmmaking techniques and discusses the effect of *Man of Aran* on the islanders, who defend Flaherty's romantic depiction of their lives. It is a curious experience to see *Man of Aran*'s "leading lady," Maggie Dirrane, some 40 and more years later.

Aside from Stoney's documentary, the making of the film was also brought to life by one of its "stars," Pat Mullen, in his 1935 autobiography, *Man of Aran*.

Man of Aran is important as Flaherty's last great documentary — although some might argue that the 1948 *Louisiana Story* holds that claim — and as the first production to illustrate the potential that Ireland holds for films outside of the travelogues dealing with the "pretty" scenery of Killarney and the Dublin countryside. While in Ireland, Flaherty was invited to make a film in Gaelic for the Irish government, *Oidhche Sheanchais*, but nothing came of the project.

It was not until 1971 that a documentary filmmaker returned to the Aran Islands, when Jim Mulkerns shot *The Return of the Islander*, a fictional short based on a true story of an Irish navvy's return to his homeland, the Aran Isles, after working on a London building site. As with *Man of Aran*, the film was acted entirely by nonprofessionals, with the exception of Maire Burke, a graduate of Galway University, who played the islander's wife. Mulkerns spent six months shooting on the islands and a further six months in editing and sound recording his film, which was commercially released by 20th Century-Fox.

Robert Flaherty was a major filmmaker with an international reputation, but there were also other, lesser American film directors who came to Ireland. One such individual was Harry Dugan of Wynnewood, Pennsylvania, who announced he was "fed up with the movie versions of comic Irishmen and other false ideas," and "set out to make a moving picture that would show the 'genuine cultural, musical and scenic beauties of the country'."[6] The result was a 1952 feature, funded by his Irish born mother, and titled *The Hills of Ireland*. Described as a "travel-musical," *The Hills of Ireland* was narrated by Pat O'Brien and featured Christopher Lynch, a protégé of John McCormack. Dugan even managed to work President Sean O'Kelly and Prime Minister Eamon De Valera into his narrative. Little wonder that Broadway columnist Walter Winchell should hail *The Hills of Ireland* as "a darlin' film."

In more recent years, the Hollywood film industry has helped Ireland economically by shooting films there as varied as Blake Edwards' *Darling Lili* (1970) and Robert Altman's *Images* (1972). Countless British sound features have been filmed in Ireland, many of them, such as David Lean's *Ryan's Daughter* (1970) and John Boorman's *Zardoz* (1974) and *Excalibur* (1981), obviously made with American money. Unfortunately, IRA terrorist threats during the making of Stanley Kubrick's *Barry Lyndon* (1975) scared away a number of potential film projects.

Ryan's Daughter is arguably the most important "foreign" film to have been produced in Ireland in recent years. The storm sequence — directed not

Using 200 Irish stone masons and thatch experts, David Lean constructed more than 40 authentic buildings on the remote tip of the Dingle Peninsula for *Ryan's Daughter*. Called Kirrary, the community lasted less than 14 months, but appeared much older.

by David Lean but by Roy Stevens, and photographed by Denys Coop — very obviously brings to mind the storm scenes from *Man of Aran*.

Set in 1916, and starring Robert Mitchum, John Mills, Trevor Howard, Christopher Jones, Sarah Miles, and Leo McKern, *Ryan's Daughter* cost some $10,000,000 to produce. Much of the money was spent in the creation of a complete Irish village of 43 stone buildings, the work of production designer Stephen Grimes (who had previously been associated with John Huston). Two hundred Irish workers were involved in the construction of the fictional village of Kirrary on the tip of the Dingle Peninsula. The site was selected by David Lean in October 1968 and the village completed by February of the following year. Additional filming took place at Inch and Banna Strand, Dunquin, Ballyferriter, and Killarney, with the production company making its headquarters in Dingle.

Twenty shareholders held grazing rights to the land on which the village was built. When filming was completed, they had the choice of retaining the village as it stood or having it demolished. Unfortunately the cost of building roads and bringing in piped water proved too expensive, and there was also

A 1927 Ford, assembled from parts found in a dozen places around the Irish countryside, becomes an English command vehicle in *Ryan's Daughter* for Christopher Jones (driving).

talk of disputes among the twenty as to who was to run the public house. As a result, the village was bulldozed back to the original rural state.

Ryan's Daughter, which was released by M-G-M, was a truly international production, but there were few Irish names among the credits, and those were limited to Irish actors such as Des Keogh, Niall Tobin, Donal Neligan, and Niall O'Brien in minor roles.

Critics in both Europe and the United States expressed disappointment with the film. Comparing David Lean's work to that of a painter, Vincent Canby in the *New York Times* (November 22, 1970) wrote, "There are in *Ryan's Daughter* a lot of canvas, paint, brushstrokes, tones and planes of vision. However, the art it represents belongs to that school of very classy calendar art supported by airlines, insurance corporations and a few enlightened barber shops. It doesn't transfigure the world. It embalms."

Before moving to Mexico, American producer/director John Huston had been a resident of the Republic of Ireland from 1952. He had filmed all or part of five features there, *Moby Dick* (1956), *The List of Adrian Messenger* (1962), *The Bible* (1966), *Casino Royale* (1967), and *Sinful Davy* (1969), and served as a figurehead in trying to persuade the Irish government to create a national film industry. In February 1973, Huston headed a group which took over Ireland's Ardmore Studios. However, John Huston moved on, and the Irish film industry had been left to flounder once again.

Back in 1933, Norris Davidson wrote in *World Film News* that "Ireland has long been regarded as the lawful prey of any English-speaking director.... There is scarcely a lake and positively no fell in Killarney that has not been pressed into service and one railway terminus in Dublin has provided Roman and Egyptian sets for English companies before now."[7] Although the American film producer has brought, and continues to bring, economic aid to the Republic of Ireland with his presence, he has never stayed long enough to help in the establishment of a true Irish national film industry. He has brought money, but he has also brought his own technicians, his own camera crew, his own grips, his own writers. Alternatively, he has found whatever additional film personnel he may require in the United Kingdom. By hiring local people as extras, he has brought employment to a depressed region, but he has not brought employment for the skilled film professional, and that is why there is no Irish film industry, why the professional Irish filmmaker must look to the United Kingdom for steady employment. Certainly the positive aspects of American filmmaking in Ireland far outweigh the negative, but a little *more* concern on the part of the American film producer in Ireland could result in a totally positive effect both for Ireland as a country and Ireland as a filmmaking entity.

III. Irish Literature and the Cinema

One of the tragedies of Northern Ireland is that the violence and bloodshed have given rise to a worldwide feeling that Ireland is no longer the land of writers but a land of terrorists and religious maniacs. In truth, the Republic of Ireland remains steeped in literary tradition. The spirits of Jonathan Swift, Richard Brinsley Sheridan, Oliver Goldsmith, Oscar Wilde, and George Bernard Shaw still permeate the Georgian squares of Dublin, although perhaps finding it slightly harder to maintain a ghostly presence among the ever-intruding high-rise buildings. Those same spirits might also be present, but certainly maintaining an uneasy foothold, in the multitude of films based upon their works.

Jonathan Swift's four-part sociological satire from 1726, *Gulliver's Travels*, has been filmed at least six times. The Russians were the first to realize its screen potential, as a piece of Communistic propaganda, and in 1935 Alexander Ptushko's *A New Gulliver* was released. The most famous version of the story is the 1939 Max Fleischer animated feature, released by Paramount. In 1959, Kerwin Mathews portrayed Gulliver in *The Three Worlds of Gulliver*, released by Columbia, which had the hero facing off against the special effects creations of Ray Harryhausen. A 1977 production featured Richard Harris as Gulliver and combined both live action and animation. Additional films include *Gulliver's Travels Beyond the Moon/Gulliver No Uchu Ryoko* (1966, Japan) and *Gulliver's Travels/Los Viajes de Gulliver* (1983, Spain).

Oliver Goldsmith (1730–1774) wrote two works which were heavily filmed during the silent era. His only novel, *The Vicar of Wakefield* (1766), was filmed some four times in the United Kingdom: in 1912, with Florence Barker; in 1913, with Violent Hopson and Chrissie White; again in 1913, with Christine Rayner; and in 1916, with Sir John Hare. The novel was also filmed twice in the United States by the Thanhouser Company of New Rochelle, New York. The first version, one reel in length, was directed by Theodore Marston, featured Frank Hart Crane, and was released in 1910. The second version was feature-length. It was directed by and starred Ernest Warde in 1917. Thanhouser also filmed a 1910, one-reel version of Goldsmith's comedy, *She Stoops to Conquer*. The play, first performed in 1773, was also filmed twice in the United Kingdom during the silent era: in 1914, with Henry Ainley and

Jane Gail, and in 1923, with Madge Stuart and Walter Tennyson. The last major production of *She Stoops to Conquer* was by the BBC in 1972, and featured Sir Ralph Richardson, Juliet Mills and Tom Courtenay.

There are no copyright problems with works from the eighteenth century, no large sums to be paid to authors for screen rights, and so, like Goldsmith, the comedies of Richard Brinsley Sheridan (1751–1816) proved equally popular with silent film producers.

Sheridan satirized the gossip and hypocrisy of fashionable society in his two masterpieces, *The Rivals* (1775) and *The School for Scandal* (1777). The former has been filmed only once in its entirety — or at least the screen concept of its entirety — in a primitive color system, Kinemacolor, in 1913. Theodore Marston directed this version, which starred William Winter Jefferson. The duel scene from the play, starring Eric Williams, was filmed in the United Kingdom in 1914. Interestingly, it was the Kalem Company which produced the only American screen version of *The School for Scandal*, in 1914, under the direction of Kenean Buel and starring Alice Joyce. Two British silent versions of the play have been filmed. The first, in 1923, was a three-reel short, with Nina Vanna as Lady Teazle and Russell Thorndike as Sir Peter Teazle. That same year, a feature-length version was released, with Queenie Thomas and Frank Stanmore in the leading roles. The latter version is chiefly of interest for the performance of Basil Rathbone as Joseph Surface. Maurice Elvey directed the only British sound version of *The School for Scandal* in 1930, with Basil Gill as Sir Peter Teazle and Madeleine Carroll as Lady Teazle.

A natural successor to Goldsmith and Sheridan in the wit and brilliance of his plays was Oscar Wilde (1854–1900), whose comedic sophistication was overshadowed by the tragedy of a private life made public. There have been more than a dozen screen adaptations of his plays, all of them of interest, and some quite superb. Wilde's 1888 fairy tale, "The Happy Prince," is one of the most recent of his works to have been filmed — as a 1974 animated short by Canadian filmmakers Murray Shostak and Michael Mills. It follows screen adaptations of some eight other works by Wilde from the heyday of his creative success in the early 1890s.

Wilde's *Lord Arthur Saville's Crime and Other Stories* (1891) was adapted to American locations for a 1943 omnibus film, *Flesh and Fantasy*, directed by Julian Duvivier. Robert Benchley held the stories together after dropping into his club to nurse a hangover. Robert Cummings and Betty Field were involved in the first story, set during Mardi Gras. Edward G. Robinson was starred in the second as a famous lawyer, warned by fortune-teller Thomas Mitchell that he is to commit a murder. Charles Boyer and Barbara Stanwyck were featured in the final tale of a tightrope performer who falls in love with a member of the audience. It is doubtful Wilde would have recognized his work, and, not surprisingly, the producer, Universal, needed three screenwriters to work on the adaptation.

It is equally doubtful that Wilde would have recognized M-G-M's 1944 adaptation of his *The Canterville Ghost*, which starred Charles Laughton as a 300-year-old ghost who had been walled up alive in his father's castle because he had been a coward on the battlefield. Margaret O'Brien was featured as an aristocratic child who instills moral fiber in an American soldier, distantly descended from the ghost, who is billeted at the castle during the Second World War. Robert Young was the soldier, and the entire production was directed by Jules Dassin.

Lady Windermere's Fan (1892), with its clever dialogue, might seem an unlikely choice for a silent film subject. Yet Warner Bros. filmed it in 1925, and thanks to Ernst Lubitsch's direction and the playing of Ronald Colman, Irene Rich and May McAvoy, it remains a delightful viewing experience to this day. The play was also filmed in the United Kingdom in 1916 (starring Milton Rosmer and Netta Westcott) and in Germany in 1935.

A work far better suited to the silent screen is Wilde's *Salome* (1893), the definitive version of which remains the one produced by and starring Alla Nazimova in 1922, under the direction of Charles Bryant (although Nazimova, apparently, left few decisions to her director). The acting is stylized as are the settings, usually credited to Natacha Rambova but more than likely, in reality, the work of art director Harold Grieve. In 1920, Hope Hampton had been *A Modern Salome*, and there was also a prestigious German version directed, also in 1922, by Robert Wiene.

A Woman of No Importance (1893) has been filmed only once, in the United Kingdom, in 1921, starring Fay Compton and Milton Rosmer. In contrast, *The Picture of Dorian Gray* has been filmed at least four times, the first being in Russia in 1915, with Vsevolod Meyerhold directing Varvara Yanova in the title role. A year later there was a British version, with Henry Victor as Gray. An atrocious German version, *Das Bildnis des Dorian Gray*, was released in 1970, with Massimo Dallamano directing Helmut Berger—good casting—in the title role, supported by Richard Todd and Herbert Lom, but it is the 1945 American production which has become, quite rightly, something of a minor classic.

M-G-M had the good sense to leave the direction and adaptation to Albert Lewin, who assembled not only a superb cast, headed by Hurd Hatfield (who is now a longtime Irish resident), George Sanders, Lowell Gilmore, Donna Reed, and Angela Lansbury (a former longtime Irish resident), but also a fine cinematographer in Harry Stradling and the famed painters Ivan and Malvin Albright to create four canvases representing the various stages in Dorian Gray's decay. The film has an elegance and style which matches Wilde's witty epigrams. Lewin made only discreet changes in the novel, and, of course, the film was much too intelligent for American audiences of the period.

It was left to the British, or at least the British studios, to produce the two other major film adaptations from the Wilde oeuvre. In 1948, Alexander Korda—a Hungarian—produced and directed *An Ideal Husband*, based on Wilde's 1895 play, which fellow Hungarian Lajos Biro adapted. Korda utilized

Technicolor in which to photograph a production featuring Paulette Goddard (who was surprisingly good), Michael Wilding, Diana Wynyard (who is always superb), Glynis Johns, Constance Collier, and Sir C. Aubrey Smith. Cecil Beaton, who had earlier been responsible for designing the costumes for a 1946 Broadway revival of *Lady Windermere's Fan*, designed the costumes for the film. (He also photographed them for an August 11, 1947, *Life* magazine layout.) It might be argued that in all of Wilde's plays there is less than meets the eye, but Alexander Korda assured that his film had enough for both the eye and the ear, with the latter not only delighting in Wilde's witticisms, but also in the music of Arthur Benjamin.

An Ideal Husband opened at New York's Roxy Theatre on January 14, 1948, and was soundly trashed by the critics. Bosley Crowther in the *New York Times* (January 15, 1948) called it "a handsome film in color with a conspicuously antiquated plot." "It could have been one of the most lusciously beautiful movies on record," commented *Time* (February 9, 1948). "Even as it stands, it is an entertaining eyeful. Unfortunately, the production occasionally becomes too slow, and too nearly a literal-minded play." *Life* (February 16, 1948) found the production "too overstuffed even for a period piece." *Newsweek* (February 2, 1948) opined that, "regarded through the microscopic intimacy of the camera, this period piece passes the lens with little more animation than so many lantern slides."

If there is one actress who remains closely associated with Oscar Wilde it is Dame Edith Evans, thanks almost entirely to her appearance as Lady Bracknell in the 1952 screen version of *The Importance of Being Earnest*, directed and adapted by Anthony Asquith from Wilde's 1895 play. Dame Edith first appeared in the role, which was to become known as her "great essay in dragonhood," in a stage production directed by and co-starring (as John Worthing) John Gielgud at London's Globe Theatre on January 31, 1939. Gielgud had, some nine years earlier, played the same role in a production featuring Mabel Terry-Lewis as Lady Bracknell, but Dame Edith quickly eclipsed all memory of the earlier actress's performance. As her biographer, director Bryan Forbes, has written, "There are few actors of my generation, male or female, who have not at some time or another, in conversation or on the stage, attempted a parody of Edith's Bracknell voice and delivery. There are some roles which live on to haunt and on occasion almost destroy an actor; Lady Bracknell was to walk Edith's battlements for the rest of her life, and even on the day of her death few commentators could resist mentioning what they (wrongly) regarded as her greatest performance."[1]

In the film version, Dame Edith was supported by a fine cast, which included Michael Redgrave, Michael Denison, Joan Greenwood, Dorothy Tutin, and Margaret Rutherford. Anthony Asquith makes no effort for naturalness in his production; this is a play and the director treats it as such, making it, along with *Long Day's Journey into Night*, one of the most sensible and intelligent of all screen adaptations of a play which does not particularly lend itself to screen adaptation. Oscar Wilde said "Nature imitates art," and Asquith appears to be in total agreement. "How glorious to see a film as good as *The Importance of Being Earnest*," commented C.A. Lejeune in *The Observer* (June 29, 1952), "in its effect so joyous; in its translation so capital; in its presentation so elegant; in its performance so distinguished; in its wit so keenly matched between the sharp line and the pungent picture!"

The film opened in New York at the Baronet Theatre on December 22, 1952, to good reviews. *Newsweek* (January 5, 1953) commented that, "Director Anthony Asquith and his players bring to this exaggerated comedy of manners the grand, artificial style that sets off perfectly the playwright's silken barbs and sharp-shod epigrams." *Time* (January 5, 1953) called it "a highly stylized, dryly amusing production." In the *New Yorker* (January 3, 1953), John McCarten wrote, "Wilde himself, I imagine, would appreciate the jauntiness with which his masterwork has been approached, and certainly he wouldn't complain about a cast that includes Michael Redgrave, Joan Greenwood, Margaret Rutherford, and Edith Evans, all of whom—particularly Miss Greenwood—enunciate his lines as if to the burnished manner born."

Although Oscar Wilde visited Los Angeles—he called it "the very edge of the great world"—there is no evidence that he ever saw a motion picture. The same, of course, is not true of George Bernard Shaw (1856–1950), who not only saw but had some very pointed remarks to make with regard to films.

Asked in 1920 what was his opinion of the average motion picture, Shaw responded, "The average motion picture play is not meant for me, so my opinion of it is not the point." As to the effect of the cinema on young and impressionable minds, he replied, "It depends on the film and on the minds. No art can have power for good without having power for evil also. If you teach a child to write, you thereby teach it to forge checks as much as to write poems."[2]

In 1925, he argued that "the silent drama is exhausting the resources of silence," and saw a future, also envisaged by J.M. Barrie, where there were more subtitles than pictures. "A play with the words left out is a play spoiled," said Shaw. "And all those filmings of plays written to be spoken as well as seen are boresome blunders except when the dialogue is so worthless that it is a hindrance instead of a help; but the moment you come to classic drama, the omission of the words and the presentation of a mere scenario is very much as if you offered as a statue the wire skeleton which supports a sculptor's modelling clay."[3]

The first film to be based on a work by George Bernard Shaw was a 1921 Czech production of *Cashel Byron's Profession* —*Roman Boxera*—produced without the author's permission. In 1927, Shaw approved a one-reel presentation of the cathedral scene from *Saint Joan*, starring Sybil Thorndike, by a British company utilizing an experimental American sound-on-film process Phonofilms. This process was later developed as Fox-Movietone sound, and, interestingly, Shaw made his first appearance before the sound camera in a Fox-Movietone newsreel, also filmed in 1927, in which he is found walking in his garden, and in the course of a rambling commentary on a variety of subjects

Michael Denison and Edith Evans in *The Importance of Being Earnest*.

offers an impersonation of Mussolini, whom Shaw described as "a most amiable man." "Having seen the summer lightning of his smile, I want to hear him thunder," commented critic Burns Mantle in the New York *Daily News*.

The first two authorized films to be based on Shaw's plays were *How He Lied to Her Husband* and *Arms and the Man*, both directed by Cecil Lewis for British International Pictures, and with Shaw providing the screenplays. They were nothing more than filmed plays, and Shaw forbade any tampering to make them palatable as motion pictures. First seen in 1931, *How He Lied to Her Husband* featured Robert Harris, Edmund Gwenn and Vera Lennox. *Arms and the Man* was released in 1932, and featured Frederick Lloyd, Maurice Colebourne, Barry Jones, and Angela Baddeley. Both films were screened at

George Bernard Shaw

the Malvern Festival, and Shaw provided defenses of the productions in the festival program — the films were poorly received by the critics and both, despite costing a minimal amount of money to produce, were financial failures.

    The next two film productions of Shaw's work were non-English. A German version of *Pygmalion* was released in 1935, directed by Erich Engel, featuring Jenny Jugo as Eliza Doolittle and Gustaf Grundgens as Professor Higgins. Ludwig Berger directed a Dutch version of the play two years later, featuring Lily Bouwmeester as Eliza and Johann de Messter as Higgins. The producers of both films were required to follow Shaw's screenplays exactly, but both, without the author's permission, attempted to make their features somewhat more cinematic. Angrily Shaw retorted, "They thought they knew better than I. If they had, they would have been Super-Shaws. As it was, they were in the position of a yokel who buys a hat for the Coronation in Piccadilly and, finding it not to his taste, brushes it the wrong way, jumps on it half-a-dozen times and then proudly walks down the street in it to show how well he knows what's in the way of gentleman's headgear."[4]

Shaw might never have agreed to another film version of his plays had it not been for a Hungarian named Gabriel Pascal to whom the playwright took an instant liking, and with whom, on December 13, 1935, Pascal began a partnership, which was to result in four films: *Pygmalion, Major Barbara, Caesar and Cleopatra,* and *Androcles and the Lion.*

The first production was also, without question, the best, co-directed by Anthony Asquith and Leslie Howard, and featuring Howard (as Professor Higgins), along with Wendy Hiller (as Eliza Doolittle), Wilfred Lawson (as Alfred Doolittle), Marie Lohr (as Mrs. Higgins), Scott Sunderland (as Colonel Pickering), and David Tree (as Freddy Eynsford-Hill). The film was shot at Pinewood Studios for a reported $675,000, and opened at the Leicester Square Theatre, London, on October 6, 1938. Shaw wrote Pascal, "You have had a tremendous triumph, on which I congratulate you and myself."

Pygmalion opened in the United States the same year as a major M-G-M release, and Shaw, much to his amusement, received the Academy Award for Best Screenplay. What Shaw and many scholars do not realize is that the version seen in the United States is not the same as that screened in the United Kingdom. Not only are the camera angles and takes different, but also the dialogue had been changed and often censored for American audiences and an entirely new music score (by William Axt replacing Arthur Honegger) provided.

Pygmalion was followed by *Major Barbara*, which began filming in 1940, with Wendy Hiller (as Major Barbara), Rex Harrison (as Adolphus Cusins), Robert Morley (as Undershaft), Robert Newton (as Bill Walker), Emlyn Williams (as Snobby Price), Sybil Thorndike (as The General), and Deborah Kerr (as Jenny Hill), under Pascal's direction. The American premiere took place at the Four Star Theatre, Los Angeles, on May 6, 1941, as a benefit for the Royal Air Force Benevolent Fund and National Bundles for Britain. "I am sending you my old plays, just as you are sending us your old destroyers," commented Shaw.

As lifeless as *Pygmalion* remained full of vitality, *Major Barbara* has not stood the test of time as well as a film, and as a stageplay it seemed dated to many 1941 critics. Writing in the *New Yorker* (May 24, 1941), John Mosher commented,

> The spirit of 1905, the revolutionary fancifulness of that particular period, is possibly as dated as *Charley's Aunt*. There is no shock now and only the mildest hint of idiosyncrasy in the millionaire's daughter who joins the

Salvation Army, and at the moment I am not entirely clear as to how we are to feel about millionaires who have made their fortunes out of munitions. The years have lulled the Shavian devilry; the audacities have a certain tea-time naughtiness about them, and there is a slight dusty, nostalgic quality in the whole thing, making it suitable for students of the drama and schoolteachers who like to keep up with things which were exciting some decades ago.

The final film for which Shaw was to provide a screenplay was *Caesar and Cleopatra*, which Pascal began directing in the summer of 1944, with a cast including Vivien Leigh (as Cleopatra), Claude Rains (as Caesar), Flora Robson (as Ftateeta), and Francis L. Sullivan (as Pothinus). Shaw was not particularly enthusiastic about Pascal's choice of *Caesar and Cleopatra*, but the British Rank Organization, which was to provide the financing, saw the production as a suitable subject for a Technicolor epic aimed at promoting British films in a postwar world. Unfortunately, the film was a critical and a box-office failure in both the United Kingdom and the United States. It lost more than $3,000,000; the J. Arthur Rank Organization commented that "*Pygmalion* was *very* profitable, *Major Barbara* adequately profitable, and *Caesar and Cleopatra* a disastrous loss."

Gabriel Pascal left England to film one final Shaw adaptation in Hollywood. *Androcles and the Lion* was produced by RKO Radio Pictures, and with Shaw's death in 1950, the screenplay was eventually prepared by Chester Erskine and Ken Englund. Erskine also directed the film, which was released in 1953, and featured Maurice Evans, Victor Mature, Alan Young, Reginald Gardiner, Jean Simmons, and Jackie the Lion. UCLA football star Woody Strode wore a lion skin for some of the sequences.

Writing in the British *The New Statesman and Nation* (October 24, 1953), William Whitebait called the production, "poor Shaw and poorer film." "It sacrifices most of the Master's satire for some blown-up spectacles of life among the Christians when the Romans were badgering them," wrote John McCarten in the *New Yorker* (January 31, 1953). *Time* (January 12, 1953) described the film as "a melancholy triumph of Hollywood spectacle and showmanship over Shavian satire and style.... This screen adaptation of a Shavian classic succeeds mostly in throwing G.B.S. to the lions."

With *Androcles and the Lion*, Gabriel Pascal's film career came to a close. His relationship with the Shaw plays continued as he tried to convert *Pygmalion* into a stage musical, but *My Fair Lady* was not to be produced until after Pascal's death.

Although the Gabriel Pascal productions were the most interesting and most important of the Shaw adaptations, there have been more than half a dozen other films based on Shaw's work since Pascal's departure from the film industry. In 1957, United Artists released Otto Preminger's version of *Saint Joan*, with a screenplay by Graham Greene, and starring Jean Seberg making her screen debut in the title role, supported by Richard Widmark, Richard

Todd, Anton Walbrook, and John Gielgud. "While there is no doubt that Mr. Preminger, who produced and directed *Saint Joan*, as well as Graham Greene, his scenarist, have a profound respect for Shaw's drama, they have not succeeded in making a motion picture out of a fine theatre piece," commented A.H. Weiler in the *New York Times* (June 30, 1957). "By cutting this three-and-a-half hour work to a little less than two hours they have not done a disservice to the dialogue. But they have failed to make obviously dramatic moments in history move a viewer."

Anthony Asquith directed two further Shaw adaptations, neither of which were in the same league as *Pygmalion*. *The Doctor's Dilemma* (1959) featured Leslie Caron, Dirk Bogarde, Alastair Sim, Robert Morley, and Felix Aylmer, and was filmed at M-G-M's British studios at Borehamwood. *Time* (January 12, 1959) reported "this modest, seldom brilliant, sometimes even repulsively cute film version of the play ... is a pertly entertaining piece of photographed theater." *The Millionairess* had already been announced for filming by Nicholas Ray in 1955 and by Preston Sturges in 1954 (with Katharine Hepburn, who had been seen in a 1953 London revival). When it was eventually filmed in 1960 by 20th Century–Fox, Asquith was the director, British writer Wolf Mankowitz had provided the screenplay, and Sophia Loren was the star, supported by Peter Sellers, Alastair Sim, Dennis Price, and Vittorio de Sica. "*The Millionairess* bears about as much resemblance to the George Bernard Shaw play on which it is based as a beanbag does to a dart," commented *Newsweek* (February 27, 1961). "Sophia Loren could not be Shaw's heroine but here that is irrelevant," wrote Stanley Kauffmann in *The New Republic* (January 30, 1961). "She is forceful, flashing, fascinating; and the picture is almost worth seeing simply to watch her wear the prodigal number of superb dresses that Balmain has made for her."

The American production company Hecht-Hill-Lancaster filmed a 1959 release of *The Devil's Disciple*, directed by Guy Hamilton, and starring Burt Lancaster, Kirk Douglas and Laurence Olivier. This first, and possibly last, screen version of Shaw's view of the American Revolution had initially been started by director Alexander Mackendrick, who quit after complaining the producers were only interested in making a swashbuckling adventure with plenty of sex. The film was received with mixed feelings by the critics, who found that Shavian wit did not mix well with adventuring.

Other screen adaptations of Shaw's plays include *Helden*, a German version of *Arms and the Man*, produced in 1958, with Franz Peter Wirth directing and starring O.W. Fischer; *Frau Warrens Gewarbe*, a German version of *Mrs. Warren's Profession*, produced in 1959, with Akos von Rathony directing and starring Lilli Palmer and O.E. Hasse. A star-studded production of *Great Catherine* was filmed in the United Kingdom in 1968, with Peter O'Toole, Zero Mostel, Jeanne Moreau, and Jack Hawkins, appearing under the direction of Gordon Flemyng. As had been proven so often in the past, no matter how major or many the stars, a Shaw screen adaptation generally did not work.

Notice should also be taken of the 1964 Warner Bros. version of *My Fair Lady*, which had first been seen on Broadway on March 15, 1956, and was adapted by Alan Jay Lerner and Frederick Loewe not so much from Shaw's play *Pygmalion* as from the 1938 screen version. George Cukor directed, and Rex Harrison, Audrey Hepburn, Stanley Holloway, Wilfrid Hyde-White, Jeremy Brett, and Gladys Cooper were the stars.

This amusing comment was supposedly made by George Bernard Shaw to Hollywood producer Sam Goldwyn: "The trouble with you, Mr. Goldwyn, is that you're interested only in art; while I'm interested only in money." Thanks to *My Fair Lady*, the Shaw estate has been receiving considerable sums of money, much of which, by the terms of the playwright's will, goes to the National Gallery of Ireland. Thus, as film historian Liam O'Leary has pointed out, moving pictures are helping to save and acquire pictures that do not move.

Dublin-born Abraham Stoker (1847–1912), better known as Bram Stoker, wrote the ultimate vampire novel, *Dracula*, which was first published in May 1897. That same year, the first stage adaptation, *Dracula or the Un-Dead*, was produced at the Royal Lyceum Theatre, London, which Stoker managed for actor Henry Irving. Transylvania might be a far cry from Ireland, but Bram Stoker created a novel whose impact is enduring, with more than 75 feature films having been based on the Dracula character. The best known, of course, is the 1931 Universal production, directed by Tod Browning, with Bela Lugosi in the title role. One other of Stoker's novels, *The Jewel of the Seven Stars* (1903), has been filmed in 1971 as *Blood from the Mummy's Tomb*, by Hammer Films. In 1973, Hammer announced plans to produce a film biography of Bram Stoker, to be called *Victim of His Imagination*, but nothing came of the company's plans.

Another Irish author, also born in Dublin, is noted for his works of horror, and that is Sheridan Le Fanu (1814–1873), a descendant, on his mother's side, of Richard Brinsley Sheridan. His novel *Uncle Silas* was adapted by Ben Travers (noted for his farces produced at the Aldwych Theatre, London), as a 1947 British feature, directed by Charles Frank, and starring Jean Simmons, Katina Paxinou, Derrick De Marney, and Derek Bond. The film, which involved the plot to drug and murder a young woman in order to gain her inheritance, was released in the United States in 1951 as *The Inheritance*.

Although Brian Friel (born 1929) has yet to see any of his works on film, his 1966 play, *The Loves of Cass McGuire*, was produced by RTE. Belfast-born (1921) Brian Moore emigrated to Canada in 1948, and it was there that his best-known novel, *The Luck of Ginger Coffey*, was filmed in 1964. The story of a husband and wife (Robert Shaw and Mary Ure) who emigrate from Ireland to Canada with their daughter (played by Libby McClintock) was well received by the critics in this Leon Roth production, directed on location in Montreal by Irvin Kershner.

Catholics: A Fable takes place after a future Vatican IV, which has outlawed the Mass in Latin and the hearing of confession. An Irish abbot (played by Trevor Howard) and his fellow priests continue to keep the old ways, and a revolutionary priest (played by Martin Sheen) is sent to put down the insurrection in the 1974 CBS "Playhouse 90" presentation of Sidney Glazier's production of Moore's novel. Jack Gold directed, and the 82-minute film was shot on location in County Tipperary, Limerick and Cork. "With *Catholics*," wrote television critic John J. O'Connor in the *New York Times*, "commercial television's aspirations to intelligence and seriousness comes of age."

Brian Moore also provided the original screenplay for Alfred Hitchcock's fiftieth feature film, *Torn Curtain*, released by Universal in 1966. The film is a minor Hitchcock opus, involving espionage and counterespionage in front of and behind the Iron Curtain. Paul Newman is cast as a United States physicist who defects to the East in order to pick the brains of an East German scientist (played by Ludwig Donath). Julie Andrews plays Newman's confused fiancée, who follows him on his trip eastward. A reasonably well-made thriller, *Torn Curtain* is marred by a semicomic sequence in which Newman attempts to kill an East German security agent, first by strangulation, then with a knife, and finally, and successfully, in a gas oven. Most critics tended to agree with Bosley Crowther in the *New York Times* (July 31, 1966) that the film was "much too slow and talky to sustain the interest for long." No one bothered to notice that Brian Moore had provided both the original story and the screenplay, and Hitchcock took credit for the original concept, claiming to have gotten the idea from the disappearance of British spies Burgess and Maclean.

In the literary tradition of James Joyce, and like Joyce before him a longtime exile from his homeland, Samuel Beckett was born in Foxrock, Dublin, on April 13, 1906. His plays were first performed at the Pike Theatre, Dublin, in a mews off Herbert Street, where Brendan Behan's plays were also first staged. In 1965, Beckett wrote the screenplay for *Film*, which was directed by Alan Schneider and produced and financed by Grove Press, publishers of *The Evergreen Review*. The New York–based publisher also acquired scripts by Harold Pinter and Ionesco, and announced plans to film them all under the working title of *Project One*. *Film*, which was photographed by Boris Kaufman and seen at both the New York and Venice film festivals, was an uncompromising, black-and-white portrait of an elderly man awaiting death in his small room. During the entire 22-minute film, the man's face was not seen, and the actor relied on his shoulders, feet and hands to convey feelings. Only in the final moment, as the man comes face to face with his own image, is he revealed as the great silent screen comedian Buster Keaton. As *Time* (September 24, 1965) commented, "The startling but quite predictable reason that *Film* scores is its sole actor: Buster Keaton." Keaton himself complained, "I don't know what the picture's about. It's so goddam arty I'm surprised the audience didn't walk out."

In addition to *Film*, Samuel Beckett's *Act Without Words II* has been adapted by Paul Joyce. It was published in *Nothing Doing* in London in 1967, but has not been filmed.

About as opposite as it is possible to be to Beckett is Henry de Vere Stacpoole (1863-1951), who was born in Kingstown (now Dun Laoghaire), just outside of Dublin. His charming Edwardian novel, *The Blue Lagoon*, has been filmed twice. There was a 1949 British version, released in the United States by Universal-International, directed by Frank Launder and starring Jean Simmons and Donald Houston. (Two Irish actors, Noel Purcell and Cyril Cusack, were featured in supporting roles.) Shot in Technicolor, the film captured much of the appeal of de Vere Stacpoole's novel of two children marooned and growing to maturity on a South Seas island. In a world weary from war, *The Blue Lagoon* was fine escapist fare. *The Hollywood Reporter* (July 28, 1949) called it "an enchanting, sensitively produced, and excellently cast English film." Far less satisfactory was the 1980 Columbia version, directed by Randal Kleiser, and starring Brooke Shields and Christopher Atkins. The screenplay by Douglas Day Stewart spent too much time on sex and sensuality and too little on charm (something which both the principals appeared to lack).

Although he was born in Brooklyn, Brian Oswald Donn-Byrne, known professionally as Donn Byrne (1889-1928), grew up in County Antrim, was educated at University College, Dublin, and always considered himself Irish. Indeed he called himself "the last traditional Irish novelist." Donn Byrne was a curious individual. He despised the United States and the Sinn Feiners. He was a staunch Orangeman who wrote—in his foreword to *Hangman's House* (1925)—of revolution as "a gallant, chivalrous adventure, in our foolish romantic hearts." It is little wonder that he was branded a "synthetic" and "professional" Irishman. What he would have made of "modern" Ireland, we will never know. In 1928 he purchased Castle Coolmaine in County Cork, and that same year he was killed in an automobile accident.

Some nine feature films are based on Donn Byrne's novels and stories: *Dangerous Hours* (1919), *The Bride's Play* (1921), *Foolish Matrons* (1921), *The Woman God Changed* (1921), *The Stranger's Banquet* (1922), *Blarney* (1926), *Hangman's House* (1928), *His Captive Woman* (1929), and *Wings of the Morning* (1937). The first is interesting in that it is a strong anti-Bolshevik drama, in which a naive socialist-leaning student becomes a Communist dupe. *Blarney* is based on a *Saturday Evening Post* story, "In Praise of John Carabine," about an Irish boxer whose fare to New York is paid by a hometown girl with an affection for him. Of course the boxer falls in love with the wife of a rival, and it takes the hometown girl to set him right. Renée Adorée and Ralph Graves were starred in this M-G-M production, directed by Marcel De Sano. *Hangman's House* is set in Ireland, and involves a girl who marries a drunken wastrel to please her father. John Ford directed this William Fox production, which starred June Collyer, Larry Kent, Victor McLaglen, and Hobart Bosworth.

The Lonely Girl (1962) by Edna O'Brien (born 1932) was filmed in 1964, with Rita Tushingham, Peter Finch and Lynn Redgrave, as the directorial debut of Desmond Davies. The screen adaptations of the plays of Sean O'Casey and John Millington Synge and the novels of Liam O'Flaherty are discussed elsewhere in this book.

Thankfully, no one has suggested filming the poetry of William Butler Yeats (1865-1939), but there are at least three films about him and his work. In 1949, a Cultural Relations Committee was formed in Ireland by Sean McBride, and its first film was *W.B. Yeats: A Tribute*. John D. Sheridan directed, Cyril Cusack provided the commentary and there are poetic selections exquisitely read by Siobhán McKenna and Micheál Mac Liammóir. Patrick Carey's *Yeats Country* (1965) is a moving tribute to both Yeats and the beauties of Ireland, with narration by Tom St. John Barry. The BBC produced a 52-minute documentary, *Horseman, Pass By*, in which Yeats' friend Frank O'Connor is seen lecturing students at Trinity College, Dublin, and remarking of Yeats' chosen epitaph, "Cast a cold eye on life, on death, horseman, pass by," that the poet never cast a cold eye on anything. The production is interesting in that it includes a recording by Yeats himself. Additionally, Yeats, without his knowledge, provided the title for the 1924 Corinne Griffith vehicle, *Black Oxen*.

James Joyce (1882-1941) had as much of a personal involvement in the motion picture as George Bernard Shaw. While teaching at the Berlitz School of Trieste, Joyce met four businessmen who controlled a couple of cinemas in the city and another one in Bucharest. He was persuaded to return to Dublin and to open a theatre there, to be followed by one in Belfast and another in Cork. Joyce found a suitable building on Mary Street, Dublin, and in November 1910, three of his colleagues arrived from Trieste to search, with Joyce, for other suitable locations in Cork and Belfast.

The projected theatres in Cork and Belfast never became reality, but on December 20, 1910, James Joyce opened Dublin's second film theatre, the Volta (named after Alessandro Volta), at 45 Mary Street, just off Sackville Street, in the heart of Dublin. Claimed as the city's first custom-built picture theatre, the Volta featured interior decoration of Italian origin, with the films accompanied by a small string orchestra.

A representative of *The Dublin Evening Telegraph* was present at the first afternoon's performance, which featured three European films, all one reel (or ten minutes) in length: *The First Paris Orphanage*, *La Pouponnière* and *The Tragic Story of Beatrice Cenci*. The last, with its depiction of the sorrowful Renaissance heroine, was too much for the newspaper which considered it "hardly as exhilarating a subject as one would desire on the eve of the festive season." There was, however, full praise for "Mr. James Joyce, who has worked indefatigably in its [the theatre's] production and deserves to be congratulated on the success of the inaugural exhibition."

As indicated by the opening day's program, the Volta tended to specialize

June Collyer, Larry Kent and Victor McLaglen in *Hangman's House*.

in short films from the Continent, particularly from France and Italy, rather than in the one-reelers produced by contemporary American companies such as Kalem, Vitagraph and American Biograph. It would be nice to claim that the Volta's selection was the result of Joyce's literary tastes, but, in reality, the choice may have been made by the writer's business partners.

Assisting Joyce in the running of the theatre was projectionist Lennie Collinge, a witty, working-class Dubliner whom the author met shortly before his death in December 1979. He was then living with his invalid wife in a two-room apartment, with shared outside lavatory, in the Kevin Street slums.

Collinge spent his entire working life as a projectionist, retiring at the age of 80 after spending his final years in that capacity with the Irish film censor. Between cups of tea, he reminisced about the Volta, which he described as "a complete fiasco." The theatre boasted only one projector, which used limelight and had no take-up spool; the film was simply allowed to run down into a bucket on the floor. While Lennie changed reels, a slide would be flashed on the screen to explain the delay. Like all projectors of this vintage, the one at the Volta was not motorized, but relied on the projectionist's cranking the handle at a uniform speed. While Lennie cranked with one hand, he would read the newspaper with the other.

James Joyce's personal problems, along with an apparent lack of business sense, led to his ceasing to be involved with the Volta in the summer of 1911. Lennie Collinge, with characteristic honesty, dismissed Joyce as a dilettante who understood nothing about films and was better off in another profession. The Volta was sold, at a loss, to Provincial Cinematograph Theatres, which, later in the decade, sold it to a Dublin company headed by Alderman J.J. Farrell and Bob O'Russ.

James Joyce continued to hold an interest in the motion picture. According to Patricia Hutchins, he was impressed with *Man of Aran* and even visited a French film studio to witness the filming of Sacha Guitry's *Pearls of the Crown*. James Joyce and the great Soviet director Sergei Eisenstein met in Paris in the winter of 1930, and the former felt that only Eisenstein or Walter Ruttman was capable of producing a film version of *Ulysses*. There was even talk of a Hungarian production of *Finnegans Wake*, and a draft scenario for the Anna Livia episode survives, written with Joyce's encouragement.[5]

Finnegans Wake, first published in 1939, was eventually filmed by New York–based experimental filmmaker Mary Ellen Bute in 1964. Based on Mary Manning's off-Broadway play, *Passages from Finnegans Wake*, the film cost $250,000 to produce, and was first seen in May 1965 at the Cannes Film Festival. Two sequences were filmed in Dublin, and the cast included Martin J. Kelly (as Finnegan), Jane Reilly (as Anna Livia Plurabelle), Peter Haskell (as Shem), and Page Johnson (as Shaun).

Joyce confidante Maria Jolas was at the Cannes screening, and was shown a copy of the trade paper *Variety*. She opined that Joyce would have liked its literary style of splintered and created words.

Finnegans Wake was not released theatrically in the United States until 1967, and then with subtitles. Paul D. Zimmerman in *Newsweek* (November 27, 1967) thought that the feature proved Joyce belonged on the bookshelf, not on film. However, *Time* (October 20, 1967) commented that "Considering the episodic quality of the film, Martin J. Kelley does remarkably well in the title role, but the other actors ornament rather than illuminate the proceedings.... Within the confines of its 94 minutes, the movie does remarkably well and remains true to Joyce by coming full cycle. It employs all the author's devices to suggest eternal recurrence; for example, it begins with the last half of a sentence and ends with the first half, leaving the words dangling in midair. In sum, re Joyce: rejoice the"

While *Finnegans Wake* was awaiting release, another Joyce adaptation was in production. *Ulysses* was written between 1914 and 1921, and first published by Sylvia Beach's famed Parisian bookshop, Shakespeare & Co. Utilizing a British film crew and a screenplay written by himself and Fred Haines, American director Joseph Strick (best known for *Muscle Beach, The Savage Eye* and *The Balcony* and soon to make *Tropic of Cancer*) began filming *Ulysses* in Dublin on July 4, 1966. The film, which cost only a reported $500,000 to produce, featured Milo O'Shea (as Leopold Bloom), Barbara

Barbara Jefford and Milo O'Shea in *Ulysses*.

Jefford (as Molly Bloom), Maurice Roeves (as Stephen Dedalus), and T.P. McKenna (as Buck Mulligan).

Strick was making a film which had already been considered and rejected as impossible to make by American producer Jerry Wald and British cinematographer-director Jack Cardiff. The director made no effort to give a period feel to his sets or locations. He filmed Dublin as it looked in 1966, not 1904.

Despite, or perhaps because of, the censorship problems which the film created both in the United States and the United Kingdom — it was banned outright in the Republic of Ireland — *Ulysses* was a considerable success at the box office, but received only mixed reviews from the critics. *Life* (March 31, 1967) commented that "It is astonishing that anyone would try to film the sprawling *Ulysses*, and even more astonishing that it has been turned into so beautifully acted and photographed a movie, one that truly reflects and actually clarifies James Joyce's cryptic masterpiece." *Time* (March 31, 1967) wrote that "the film he [Joseph Strick] has made is hardly the mighty epic Joyce imagined. In a show-business sense it is only a little old black-and-white movie, brought in for less than $1,000,000 and played by a group of actors no better known in the U.S. than any man jack in the Dublin telephone directory. It

Fionnula Flanagan and Chris O'Neill in *James Joyce's Women*.

offers the spectator about as much of Joyce's chaffering, all-including most farraginous chronicle' as a two-hour stopover at Shannon would offer him of Ireland. It is honest, mildly sensational, and for the most part intelligent: a pictorial precis of the novel that may not be the best but is certainly far from the worst movie version imaginable."

In 1970, John Huston announced plans to film *Portrait of the Artist as a Young Man*, which Joyce first published in book form in 1916, to be adapted by Hugh Leonard. However, it was left again to Joseph Strick to bring the autobiographical novel to the screen in a 1977 version, filmed the previous year entirely on location in Ireland. Judith Rascoe provided the screenplay, and the cast included Bosco Hogan (as Stephen Dedalus), T.P. McKenna (as Simon Dedalus), John Gielgud (as preacher), Rosaleen Linihan (as May Dedalus), and Maureen Potter (a superb comedienne whose variety shows at the Gaiety Theatre were the highspots of the Dublin years, as Dante).

The film received its world premiere at the Curzon Theatre, Dublin, in October 1977, the first of Joseph Strick's films to be approved by the Irish censor. Strick had made every effort to shoot on the locations mentioned by Joyce,

A Dublin street scene from Kieran Hickey's *Faithful Departed*.

including Belvedere and Bewley's Cafe, a Dublin institution. The Irish audience was somewhat perturbed by the film's slow pace. American critics were fairly subdued in their commentary. "*Portrait of the Artist as a Young Man* is both worthy and maddening," wrote Vincent Canby in the *New York Times* (April 22, 1979). "It's worthy because Mr. Strick and his screen writer, Judith Rascoe, obviously admire Joyce enough to wish to share that admiration with a large cinema audience, and they have packed the film with great passages of the Joycean language. It's maddening because their task is an impossible one, as it was when Mr. Strick made his equally faithful, equally frustrating screen version of *Ulysses*." In *New York* magazine (April 31, 1979), John Simon commented, "As an appetite whetter for potential readers of the novel, the film might just do. As a work of art in its own right, never."

Fionnula Flanagan had appeared, in the role of Gerty MacDowell, in the film version of *Ulysses*. She had also appeared as Molly Bloom in Burgess Meredith's 1973 Broadway production of *Ulysses in Nighttown*, which co-starred Zero Mostel. Because of these roles, and her Irish background, Flanagan decided to develop a one-woman show, in which she would appear as six of James Joyce's women — three from his books and three from his own life. The result was *James Joyce's Women*, directed by Burgess Meredith, and first seen at the South Coast Repertory Theatre, Costa Mesa, California, in August 1977.

In 1982 a television special was planned, but because of legal complications, Fionnula Flanagan decided to recreate her production as a film. The result, still called *James Joyce's Women*, and filmed entirely on location in and around Dublin, was released in the spring of 1985. Michael Pearce directed, and Timothy E. O'Grady and Chris O'Neill headed a supporting cast of some 14 players. Flanagan appeared as Nora Barnacle Joyce, Sylvia Beach, Harriet Shaw Weaver, Gerty MacDowell, the Washerwoman, and Molly Bloom, delivering the last's sensual soliloquy in the nude. Unfortunately, the viewer is all too aware that Ms. Flanagan is an actress—a very good one—and she is only acting out a series of parts. As Janet Maslin noted in the *New York Times* (September 12, 1985), the elements in the film "are united more by her presence as an actress than by their ability to evoke Mr. Joyce's character or his greatness."

James Joyce is also remembered in at least three documentaries, the best of which is *Faithful Departed* (1968), a ten-minute short produced by Kieran Hickey. The director evokes the Dublin of June 16, 1904, the date on which *Ulysses* is set, through the use of photographs compiled by the company of William Mervyn Lawrence during the late nineteenth and early twentieth centuries. The music is taken from songs referred to in *Ulysses*, and the commentary spoken by Jack MacGowran. *Joyce's Dublin* (1967), produced and directed by Norman Cohen, a companion film to *Brendan Behan's Dublin* and 20 minutes in length, is best recalled for its narration by Micheál Mac Liammóir, and the reading of Joyce's words by Ulick O'Connor. Andy O'Mahoney narrates the ten-minute short *City of James Joyce* (1968) produced by Bill St. Leger, whose title tells it all.

"You have disgraced yourselves again" was the shouted remark of W.B. Yeats to the Abbey Theatre audience, following the 1926 premiere of Sean O'Casey's *The Plough and the Stars*—as Micheál Mac Liammóir so aptly put it, "the sensibilities of Mr. Hyde in rage at not seeing Dr. Jekyll's face in the mirror."[6] It is a comment which, surprisingly, should not really be directed too frequently at those filmmakers who have tackled screen adaptations of the works of Ireland's greatest authors, from Oliver Goldsmith to George Bernard Shaw.

IV. The Irishman in Hollywood

Just as on each St. Patrick's Day every red-blooded American becomes a green-adorned Irishman, so have many in the film industry claimed Irish ancestry. The reason is as befuddled as the reason why the average American feels duty-bound to wear green in honor of St. Patrick. Columbus Day does not evoke the same feeling of solidarity with the Italian people, nor has a sizeable number in the film industry claimed Italian ancestry. The poor British do not even have an American parade of their own. Yet the British remain one of the United States' staunchest allies and a leading member of NATO, while the Republic of Ireland remains outside of that organization and has never expressed unilateral support for any American action. Indeed, during the Second World War, the Republic of Ireland retained absolute neutrality to the extent that in May of 1945, Eamon de Valera visited the German legation in Dublin to offer his condolences upon hearing of the death of Adolf Hitler (one of the most shameful days in modern Irish history).

Yet most in Hollywood seek an Irish connection. There is Anthony Quinn, claiming Irish-Mexican parentage; in reality, not that unusual considering the number of Irish who emigrated to Mexico at the turn of the century. At one time, Mary Pickford claimed that she replaced her real name of Gladys Smith with a name from one of her Irish ancestors.

In 1918, *Photoplay* published an article on film performers of Irish ancestry, noting that the Irish "propel the production side of the photoplay business even as Wilsonian Democracy propels the civilized world."[1] Among the Irishmen and women whom *Photoplay* found in Hollywood were John, Lionel and Ethel Barrymore, J. Warren Kerrigan, Francis X. Bushman, Thomas Meighan, William and Dustin Farnum, Crane Wilbur, Mae Murray, female impersonator Julian Eltinge, Olive Thomas, George M. Cohan, Mae Marsh, Mack Sennett, Texas Guinan, Dorothy Dalton, Molly Malone, Mabel Normand, Ruth Roland, Belle Bennett, Enid Markey, Bessie Love, Geraldine Farrar, Tom Mix, Robert Harron, Charles Ray, Jack Mulhall, and even Dorothy and Lillian Gish. And yet not one of these performers was born in Ireland and few had parents born on the Emerald Isle.

One of the most suave and debonair of screen actors during both the silent and sound eras was Adolphe Menjou. In his autobiography, *It Took Nine*

Tailors, he wrote: "Mother was born in the village of Letterfrach in the picturesque Connemara district of County Galway, Ireland. For many years she thought a theatre was just a way station on the road to perdition. Her maiden name was Nora Joyce and she was a distant cousin of James Joyce, the novelist. But after struggling through the first hundred pages of *Ulysses*, she disclaimed the relationship."

The professional Irishman could feel right at home in the American film industry in that Hollywood has continued the image of the stage Irishman through to the present. These professional Irishmen have their origins in the stereotypical Irish actors of the nineteenth century. Their presence was first felt on stage through the plays of Dion Boucicault and the music of Victor Herbert (whose life was filmed by Paramount in 1939, as *The Great Victor Herbert*, with Walter Connolly in the title role). In the early years of this century, Ernest R. Ball (1878–1927) kept the popular image of Ireland and the Irish alive with such songs as "When Irish Eyes Are Smiling," "A Little Bit of Heaven" and "Mother Machree." He toured the vaudeville theatres of America from 1911 onwards, and in 1944 a film of his life, *Irish Eyes Are Smiling*, was produced by 20th Century-Fox, with Dick Haymes portraying Ball. The original Tyrone Power (1797–1841) was one of the greatest of stage Irishmen both in the United Kingdom (where it has been argued that the stereotype originated in an effort to explain the behavioral patterns of England's neighbor across the water) and in the United States. His grandson, Tyrone Power, was often cast as an "Irishman" on screen, in films such as *Second Honeymoon* (1937), *In Old Chicago* (1938), *The Razor's Edge* (1946), *The Luck of the Irish* (1948), and *The Long Gray Line* (1955). He was also selected by John Ford to introduce the three stories comprising *The Rising of the Moon* (1957).

With the coming of the twentieth century, the stage or professional Irishman became an embarrassment to the theatre. There is a cartoon which appeared in the January 5, 1922, issue of the old humor magazine *Life* showing an actor marked as "professional Irishman," surrounded by such items as "Hibernian Cream," a coat marked "Ancient Wrongs" and a poster for *"To Hell with England*, a great hit." He is asking the theatre page boy, "Take my act off? Then how am I to make a living?" These professional Irishmen were reminders to a portion of the theatre audience, growing steadily sophisticated, of its origins, origins which it was trying to overcome. After all, what had the Irish actually brought to the United States as they sought to escape the poverty of their homeland? The answer, in part, is political corruption and ardent and often repressive Roman Catholicism, hardly anything of which to boast.

Thus, while the stage moved forward and away from its past of racial stereotypes (which also prominently included Jews and blacks), the fledgling film industry embraced such stereotypes for its productions. The audience for the motion picture was far less sophisticated, definitely working class, when compared to that for the stage. It demanded and appreciated what the theatre, with its new-found legitimacy of purpose, could no longer offer.

The motion picture could provide a wide range of Irish characters: priests, smiling colleens, heavy-drinking and heavy-fighting rogues, adventurers, gangsters, and many more. American-born James Cagney was to alternate as professional Irish gangsters and professional Irish cops. British-born Victor McLaglen represented the boozing Irish bully, often in the role of a soldier as evidenced by such films as *Wee Willie Winkie* (1937), *She Wore a Yellow Ribbon* (1949), and *Fort Apache* (1950). *Mother Machree* and *Hangman's House*, both released in 1928, had established him as a screen Irishman, and that characterization was more than legitimized with McLaglen's portraying Gypo Nolan in *The Informer* (1935), for which he received the Academy Award for Best Actor.

Australian-born Errol Flynn was the typical Irish adventurer, notably in *Captain Blood* (1935), which is set in the 1680s, with Flynn as an Irish nobleman serving as a slave on an Englishman's West Indian plantation — and what could be more stereotypical than that? Of course Irish priests proliferate in American films, with Bing Crosby, Spencer Tracy and Barry Fitzgerald (the only genuine Irishman in the bunch) taking the lead. The family unit is often portrayed as Irish, notably in *A Tree Grows in Brooklyn* (1945), with its Irish-American cast including James Dunn (seen a year earlier in *Leave It to the Irish*), Lloyd Nolan, James Gleason, and J. Farrell MacDonald. The family unit is also an integral part of *How Green Was My Valley* (1941), which, despite its Welsh background, is decidedly Irish in both casting and performance. Perhaps because of the negative qualities inherent in Irish-American politics (after all many Irish-American politicians were among those who sought to keep the United States out of the Second World War for as long as possible and in so doing probably aided the war effort, at least temporarily, of Nazi Germany), the Irish politician has never held a strong place in American films, with the obvious exception of Spencer Tracy in *The Last Hurrah* (1958). Mention should also be made of Cliff Robertson as America's folk-hero "Irish" President John F. Kennedy in *PT-109* (1963). Then, there is the Irish cowboy, epitomized by the all-American John Wayne, most of whose characters have had Irish-American backgrounds.

Americans Patsy Kelly and Marjorie Main represent the hard-boiled, wise-cracking Irish-American female. Unfortunately, the latter's *Mrs. O'Malley and Mr. Malone* (1950) never became the successful series as did *Ma and Pa Kettle* (1949). These two could portray maids, sidekicks (to either men or other women), and tough broads with hearts of gold. They and their male counterparts were once the safest casting elements in a Hollywood film. They were as American as apple pie and as Irish as a shamrock. Their appeal was guaranteed, and their presence promised money, lots of it, at the box office.

The best known of Hollywood's professional Irishmen was Pat O'Brien (1899–1983), who studied acting in company with his friend Spency Tracy at the American Academy of Dramatic Arts and had his first major success in Hollywood as reporter Hildy Johnson in the 1931 film of *The Front Page*. A year later, O'Brien signed a long-term contract with Warner Bros., becoming a member of its so-called "Irish Mafia," a group of actors which included Spencer Tracy, Frank McHugh, Allen Jenkins, Frank Morgan, James Gleason, Robert Armstrong, and James Cagney.

In 1938, O'Brien played a screen priest for the first time, opposite Cagney in *Angels with Dirty Faces*. He also played a priest opposite Cagney in *The Fighting 69th* (1940). His last screen appearance, again with Cagney, was as a defense lawyer in *Ragtime* (1981). When asked if he was underrated as an actor, O'Brien replied, "*Me!* I'm damn good and I know it; I pride myself on one thing and that's timing, and I have experience enough to play both comedy and drama at the same time. And if that isn't a burst of ego, I don't know what is."[2]

Pat O'Brien's portrayals of Irish-Americans are legendary, and include Colonel Ryan in *Bombardier* (1943) and the title role in *Fighting Father Dunne* (1948). His classic Irish-American portrayal is that of the Notre Dame coach in *Knute Rockne — All American* (1940), who exhorts his team to "win one for the Gipper."

It was natural that O'Brien should have worked with John Ford, of whom he told Scott Eyman,

> Ford was the genius of them all. He was an artist drawing a portrait in oil, with [Frank] Capra a close second. I made *Air Mail* for Jack Ford in '32 and he was wonderful with me, but he got a little prickly over the years. He was always a very rough disciplinarian; I remember on *The Last Hurrah* he'd go nuts about the littlest things, like marks on the floor. But after the storm, he'd be the same old Jack. He would never talk the part you were playing, he'd just tell you what he wanted. "I hope you can get it," he'd say, chewing on that handkerchief he always had. When you failed, he'd say, "That wasn't what I wanted. Try to get what I wanted. We're going to take another whack at it and it better be good." After you finally got it, he'd come over and put his arms around you. "Why the hell didn't you get it in the first place?" he'd say.[3]

If Pat O'Brien was the quintessential professional Irishman in front of the camera, John Ford (1895–1973) was the quintessential professional Irishman behind the camera. The son of Irish immigrants from Galway, who met and married in the United States, John Ford was born Sean Augustine Feeney. (Ford always claimed his real name was Sean Aloysius O'Feeney.) His brother Francis first adopted the name Ford, and when he began his career, John followed suit. As indicated by his famous quote, "My name's John Ford. I make Westerns," much of the director's career, particularly in the early years, was taken up with the Western genre, but Ford has displayed a predilection for films with Irish themes that can be dated back to 1915, when he appeared in *The Doorway of Destruction*, directed by his brother, Francis, for Universal, and concerned with an Irish regiment saving the day for the British during the Sepoy Rebellion. The first film with an Irish theme that Ford directed himself

John Ford

Leslie Fenton and Janet Gaynor in *The Shamrock Handicap*.

was *The Shamrock Handicap,* a 1926 William Fox production starring Janet Gaynor, J. Farrell MacDonald, and Leslie Fenton, which involved an Irish group coming to the United States, winning a horse race, and returning in glory to the old country.

In 1928, Ford directed a screen adaptation of Donn Byrne's *Hangman's House*, a William Fox production, starring Victor McLaglen, Hobart Bosworth, June Collyer, and Larry Kent. It is a story of an Irish patriot who returns home to kill the man who married and deserted his sister. In the book, Byrne writes "A Foreword to Foreigners," which must have appealed to Ford in its evocation of a land of dreams which, at this point, he had yet to visit:

> I am certain that no race has for its home the intense love we Irish have for Ireland. It is more than love. It is a passion. We make no secret of it,

and people gibe at us, saying, with a sneer that does not speak well of their manners, "Why don't you go back to Ireland?" Which is not merited, for every one must know the intricate prison this life is, and how this friendship, that grave, and even the unutterable vulgarity of money matters tie us to an alien land. So that to many millions of us, and a million's sons and daughters, Ireland must be a land of dreams. We are like the children who listen about a nursery fire to a tale out of Grimm or Hans Andersen. But the children grow up, and they know—God help them!—that there was never a Cinderella, who had a magic coach, or king's daughters who danced away their slippers among enchanted trees, but our Ireland, we know, did and does live. Gentle and simple, we have all our memories, the hunt ball or the cross-roads dance. Surely there was never such gaiety, such music.[4]

It is this vision of Ireland as a never-never land which permeates so much of John Ford's work. He never viewed Ireland as it is, or as it was, but as a land of his dreams. As one Dubliner once remarked to me of John Ford's films, "He sees Ireland through the eyes of a leprechaun." His vision of Ireland was that of a poet, but a decidedly second-rate poet, whose view was often patronizing and boorish. Perhaps John Ford looked upon his parents as Irish peasants and could never accept that the Irish in the twentieth century could be anything more. Long after the British had left, John Ford's Ireland was still running according to a British class system, with the "peasants" doing anything possible to frustrate their "masters" (as witness the "A Minute's Wait" sequence in *The Rising of the Moon*).

Lindsay Anderson once wrote that "Ford has no time for the English," which irritated Ford, who responded, "I've got more British than I have American friends.... Of course, you must remember I'm Irish—we have a reputation to keep up."[5] John Ford *was* an enigma. By all accounts, he supported the IRA. At the same time, he maintained close friendships with a number of Britishers in Hollywood, notably Alan Mowbray and Anna Lee (who might well be regarded as a professional "English Lady," resolutely flying the Union Jack in front of her West Hollywood home and denouncing IRA terrorism in Ulster). Yet if John Ford built up various images to the frustration of interviewers, he remained constant in his dated and unrealistic view of Ireland and the Irish.

Ford cast veteran stage actor J. Farrell MacDonald (1875–1952) as Aloysius Riley, a hard-drinking, New York Irish-American police officer in *Riley the Cop* (1928). MacDonald became a stereotypical Irish-American for John Ford, appearing in leading roles in many of the director's silent films and in supporting roles in a number of talkies.

Liam O'Flaherty's novel *The Informer* was first filmed in 1929 by British International Pictures, with an American-born director of German parentage, Arthur Robison, a Hungarian leading lady, Lya de Putti, and a Swedish leading man, Lars Hanson. The result is a film which is superbly gripping, and which illustrates the director's schooling in German expressionism.

John Ford (sitting) directing Victor McLaglen in *The Informer*.

Unfortunately, the silent film was also released in a sound version in which the Irish heroine spoke (or to be more precise was dubbed) like a young lady from South Kensington, and the working-class Irish spoke with cultured Oxford accents!

John Ford's version for RKO came six years later, and won for him the first of four Academy Awards for Best Director. The film also received Academy Awards for Best Actor (Victor McLaglen), Best Music (Max Steiner) and Best Writing (Dudley Nichols). The last should, perhaps, have been shared with Ford, for the two men worked closely on the script while cruising on Ford's yacht off the Mexican coast. Certainly McLaglen gives the best performance of his career as Gypo Nolan, who betrays his friend to the British authorities in Dublin for a £20 reward. Playing opposite McLaglen, British actress Margot

Una O'Connor (left) and Eileen Crowe in *The Plough and the Stars*.

Grahame—making her American film debut—lacks the necessary credentials to play Irish tragedy. Although the film is well made and intelligently produced, *The Informer* fails to come to grips with the political situation in Ireland and seems to go out of its way to avoid controversy. (Despite this, the film was initially banned in the then–Irish Free State.)

Plans were announced in April 1965 for a Broadway musical to be based on the film, with music and lyrics by Burton Lane and E.Y. Harburg. Tyrone Guthrie was announced as director, but, thankfully, nothing came of the project.

The Irish government did not approve of John Ford's *The Informer*. Nor did it approve of Sean O'Casey's *The Plough and the Stars*, with its highly personal interpretation of the 1916 rebellion. Although Ford's version of the O'Casey play was approved for screening in the Irish Free State, the government would have done better to ban it as a travesty of a great play by a great man. Screenwriter Dudley Nichols expanded the roles of the young lovers, Nora and Jack Clitheroe, to the detriment of O'Casey's dialogue and the myriad of small parts which make the play shine. As the British critic James Agate wrote in the *Sunday Times* (February 17, 1937), "O'Casey's play is crammed full of magnificent prose poetry; there isn't a line of any kind of prose or poetry in the film. If I be confuted by passages taken boldly from the play I shall retort that they have lost so much savour in filming that they have become unrecognizable."

Dudley Nichols' screenplay keeps alive Jack Clitheroe, and in order that the film may end on a tragic note introduces James Connolly, leader of the Irish Citizen Army (played by Moroni Olsen), who is executed. As Nora, Barbara Stanwyck emotes too much, while Preston Foster, as Jack Clitheroe, is wooden and unappealing. (Unfortunately, Ford was not permitted to cast, as he had wished, Spencer Tracy, in the leading role.) What *The Plough and the Stars* does offer is magnificent ensemble performances by members of the Abbey Theatre Company: Barry Fitzgerald, Denis O'Dea, Eileen Crowe, F.J. McCormick, Arthur Shields, and (not strictly a member of the Company) Una O'Connor. As Bessie Burgess, Eileen Crowe's droning voice is fascinatingly captivating, while—for once in his Hollywood career—Barry Fitzgerald proves why Sean O'Casey labelled him "the greatest comic actor in the world."

RKO executives were disappointed in the film that Ford had produced, and prior to its general release in 1937, additional scenes, involving Stanwyck and Foster, were photographed by George Nicholls, Jr. Also, a considerable amount of (admittedly fascinating) newsreel footage of the Easter Rebellion and the later Civil War was added.[6] The film was far from successful, proving that *Variety* (February 3, 1937) was correct in questioning "to what extent the American public is interested in Ireland's troubles."

Although they are not "Irish" films, John Ford's *The Long Voyage Home* (1940) and *How Green Was My Valley* (1941) deserve mention here. The first, based on plays by Eugene O'Neill, who is of Irish ancestry, contains Irish-American characters, played by, among others, J.M. Kerrigan and Arthur Shields. The latter could do no wrong as far as Ford was concerned and was known contemptuously as "John Ford's white-headed boy." *How Green Was My Valley* might just as well have been set in Ireland (if Ireland had been a coal-mining country) as in Wales. The film is dominated by Sara Allgood, and other Irish players include Maureen O'Hara, Barry Fitzgerald and Arthur Shields.

Ford returned to Ireland with a vengeance with his 1952 release of *The Quiet Man*. Filmed on location in Galway and Connemara with additional scenes filmed at the Republic Studios in Studio City, California (despite Ford's original intention of filming interiors in Italy, of all places), *The Quiet Man* features John Wayne as an American returning to his birthplace and winning the hand of Irish colleen Maureen O'Hara. Rather charmingly, Eileen Crowe (who played Mrs. Elizabeth Playfair in the film) remembered O'Hara as "a beautiful creature, but she couldn't act."

As A.H. Weiler wrote in the *New York Times* (August 31, 1952), Ford "is in love with an ideal he has cherished and he makes no effort to hide the fact that his heart is on his sleeve and that it has shaped him and his films." Unfortunately, while filming his Irish ideal, John Ford is also highly patronizing in his approach to a people who are far more complicated than might at first appear to the casual observer. John McCarten in the *New Yorker* (August 23, 1952) quite rightly pointed out that in Ford's Ireland everybody "is just as cute as a button. The people are not only cute but quaint, and the combination stretched out for something more than two long hours, approaches the formidable.... *The Informer* appears to have fallen into a vat of treacle."

Unfortunately, there was worse to come. In 1955, Ford participated in the creation of an Irish film company, Four Provinces Films, Ltd. (in a reference to the four Irish provinces of Ulster, Munster, Connaught, and Leinster), with Lord Michael Killanin (who was chairman), Michael Scott, and Brian Desmond Hurst. In March of 1956, Ford began directing the company's first feature, *Three Leaves of a Shamrock*, which was to be released the following year by Warner Bros. as *The Rising of the Moon*. Introduced by Tyrone Power, the feature consisted of three short episodes: "The Majesty of the Law" by Frank O'Connor, "A Minute's Wait" by Michael J. McHugh, and "The Rising of the Moon" by Lady Gregory. The first, featuring Noel Purcell, Cyril Cusack and Jack MacGowran, is plain boring. The second is a typical Fordian view of Irish incompetence, which offers wonderfully comic performances by Jimmy O'Dea and Maureen Potter. The third bears almost no resemblance to Lady Gregory's play, but does offer a superb performance by Eileen Crowe, playing the role of the police sergeant's wife, a part Lady Gregory had not written. The final sequence was filmed in part at the Spanish Arch in Galway City.

Yet again, John McCarten in the *New Yorker* (July 20, 1957) summed it up succinctly when he wrote, "There can be no doubt that Mr. Ford dearly loves the Irish, but I'm not at all sure that in his excess of affection he hasn't been guilty of representing them as superficially as if they were all straight out of vaudeville." *The Rising of the Moon* received its world premiere at the Metropole Theatre, Dublin, in June 1957, opening in the United States for the first time at the 55th Street Playhouse on July 15, 1957. It took a while, but eventually emotions were aroused in Ireland by the production. In February 1958, D.P. Quish of the Limerick County Council attacked *The Rising of the Moon* as "a vile production and a travesty of the Irish people." The Council requested the Irish Justice Minister to contact all countries with which the Republic had diplomatic relations to demand that the film be withdrawn from circulation. There was no official response to the Limerick County Council's demands.

John Ford's final involvement with Ireland came in 1964 when he began work on the direction of *Young Cassidy* for Metro-Goldwyn-Mayer and Sextant Films. Based on Sean O'Casey's early life as revealed in his autobiography, *Mirror in My House*, the film starred Rod Taylor (as Sean Cassidy), Maggie Smith (as Nora), Julie Christie (as Daisy Battles), and Flora Robson (as Mrs. Battles), and was shot on location in Ireland. Because the producers would not agree to end the film as Ford had wished, the director became conveniently ill, and

John Ford (right) directing Eileen Crowe in *The Rising of the Moon*.

was replaced by cinematographer-turned-director Jack Cardiff (who had been responsible for the Technicolor photography on *Wings of the Morning*).

Ford may have been nothing more than a professional Irishman-director, but Ireland has produced three honest-to-goodness Irish directors who made names for themselves during the silent era. Additionally, the country gave birth to a major British director, who also worked in Hollywood.

William Desmond Taylor (1869–1922) was born William Cunningham Deane Tanner in Carlow, County Cork. His biggest claim to fame is not that he was a director of any major talent, but that he had the misfortune (as far as his life was concerned) and the good fortune (as far as his lasting notoriety is concerned) to have been murdered in one of the greatest of Hollywood's unsolved mysteries, with his murderess apparently being Mrs. Charlotte Selby, the mother of actress Mary Miles Minter. An actor on both stage and screen before becoming a director in 1914, Taylor was not an accomplished director, despite the claims by Irish film historians. Those of his films which survive indicate that he was little more than competent, although he does have to his credit the direction of a number of important Paramount features of the late 'teens, such as *Tom Sawyer* (1917), *Johanna Enlists* (1918), *Anne of Green Gables* (1919), and *Huckleberry Finn* (1920).

Herbert Brenon (1880–1958) was born in Dublin, grew up in London and began his working life as an office boy in Pittsburgh, Pennsylvania. After experience in the theatre, he joined Carl Laemmle's IMP Company and directed his first film in 1912. Brenon became one of the better and more versatile directors of the silent era, although, apparently, he had quite an Irish temper, and Lillian Gish once told me that she was advised by Douglas Fairbanks and Mary Pickford not to consider working for him. In the 'teens years, he directed Theda Bara in *The Kreutzer Sonata* and *The Two Orphans*, both released in 1915; Annette Kellermann in *Neptune's Daughter* (1914) and *A Daughter of the Gods* (1916); and Alla Nazimova in *War Brides* (1916). Under contract to Famous Players-Lasky/Paramount during most of the twenties, Brenon directed *Peter Pan* (1924), starring Betty Bronson in the title role and, making her film debut, Irish-American Mary Brian as Wendy. He also directed another J.M. Barrie fantasy, *A Kiss for Cinderella* (1926), as well as the first screen adaptation of *The Great Gatsby* (1926) and the first screen version of *Beau Geste* (1926).

The director proved equally capable during the sound era, spending the second half of the thirties in the United Kingdom, where he directed, among others, the memorable *The Housemaster* (1938). By all accounts, Brenon never particularly considered himself an Irishman; his accent, dapper attire and love of J.M. Barrie's works characterized him more as an English gentleman.

Thanks largely to the efforts of Liam O'Leary, who has written the definitive (and only) book on his life and career, Rex Ingram (1893–1950) is probably now regarded as Ireland's greatest home-grown director. Born Reginald Ingram Montgomery Hitchcock in Dublin, the director was a fairly colorful character, none of whose films indicate an Irish background or the upbringing of the son of a Protestant minister. He left Ireland for the United States in 1911 and never returned.

Active as a director from 1916 through 1932, Rex Ingram's films are pictorially impressive, but often lack vitality. He is a director more interested in the total scene, its look and composition, rather than what is happening within the scene. While some of his features, notably *The Four Horsemen of the Apocalypse* (1921), which made of Rudolph Valentino a star, are deserving of the appellation "classic," others tend to be almost dreary in comparison. It is perhaps not surprising that Ingram should have made only one all-sound feature, *Baroud* (1932), and it did almost nothing for his career, although it is at least amusing to watch Ingram appearing in a leading role as a French officer in Morocco, complete with a very strong Irish accent.

Poor Herbert Wilcox (1892–1977) always gets short shrift from Irish film historians, despite his having been born in Cork. Perhaps it is because all of his films are so defiantly pro-British, glorifying Empire and the English social life. Certainly it is strange to consider that an Irishman should have been responsible for *Victoria the Great* (1937), *Sixty Glorious Years* (1938), and such wonderful exercises in British middle-class frivolity as *Spring in Park Lane* (1948) and *Maytime in Mayfair* (1949).

In his autobiography, Wilcox writes of serving in the British army during the First World War, and being shot by an Irish bullet in Fermoy, County Cork, in 1916. With a strange negative pride, he tells that "the first shot in Fermoy killed the great young hero of Cork County. He was their 'Michael Collins.' The second bullet hit me."[7]

There is one other director deserving of mention, and that is Roy William Neill (1886–1946), who was born either in Dublin, or, more likely, on board a ship off the Irish coast. He began his film career in 1915, initially as an actor with producer Thomas Ince, and shortly thereafter becoming a director. He was active in the British film industry in the late thirties and returned to the United States to produce and direct the popular Sherlock Holmes series of films, starring Basil Rathbone and Nigel Bruce, released by Universal. He died in London while negotiating the production of an independent feature to be shot in England and Ireland.

Irishman Creighton Hale will always be an integral part of the silent cinema. He could always be relied upon to give a competent, if sometimes lackluster, performance, whether it be as Pearl White's man Friday in *The Exploits of Elaine* or the bungling hero of *The Cat and the Canary*.

He was born Patrick Fitzgerald in Cork on May 24, 1892. His father was an Irish singer and actor who would tour the country with his own repertory company. The young Hale, naturally, followed in his father's footsteps, making his first stage appearance at the age of five. However, Hale's stage career was interrupted by his parents' decision to send their son to be educated in England. Upon leaving school, he took up engineering, then journalism, but eventually returned to his first love, the stage.

In 1909, while appearing with Lady Forbes Robertson's stage company, Hale went to the United States, and like many Irishmen before and since decided to stay there. It was House Peters, a popular film player of the 'teens who suggested that Creighton Hale try his luck in films. "Peters oozed prosperity," Hale later recalled in a fan magazine interview. "His overcoat was of the latest cut, his hat obviously new, and he wore yellow gloves. I asked him if he had found a gold mine. 'No,' replied Peters in a ponderous manner. 'I'm playing in pictures'."

Hale's entry into films was far from auspicious; he started as an extra with the East Coast–based Pathé Company. It was apparently Pathé director Frank Powell who realized Hale's potential, and picked him to be Pearl White's leading man in *The Exploits of Elaine* and *The Romance of Elaine*. Hale's mild-mannered playing provided a perfect foil to the heroics of serial star Pearl White. "We worked very hard day after day," recalled the cinema's latest leading man. "I usually left my house at 7:00 a.m., and drove my little old motor car to the studio at Jersey City. We worked steadily all day, coming home any hour at night, sometimes so utterly fagged out that I'd fall asleep at the wheel, and catch myself just in time making a bee-line for an obstructive lamp-post!"

In 1916, Frank Powell invited Creighton Hale to appear in the interesting production of *Charity*, based on an idea by Linda Arvidson (Mrs. D.W. Griffith), who appeared along with Sheldon Lewis—also from the Pearl White serials—and Zena Keefe in this supposed exposé of corrupt orphan asylums. *Charity* had a very checkered existence. It was originally produced with money from a wealthy New York brewer, who was later forced to withdraw his support following criticism of the project by various religious groups. It was first released in September of 1916 and was a dismal failure; two years later the film was reissued by the Mutual Company and again flopped. It was last reincarnated in 1920, reedited and retitled, and yet again it flopped.

In private life, Creighton Hale was a quiet, unassuming sort of a person. He was considered one of the best dressed leading men of the silent era. Although generally cast as a typical English "type," Hale was proud of his Irish upbringing, although he was never allowed to play an Irishman on the screen. His two marriages, to Victoria Lowe and Kathleen E. Beering, both ended in divorce.

Between 1919 and 1921, Creighton Hale was a member of D.W. Griffith's stock company of actors, based at the Mamaroneck Studios just outside of New York. Hale appeared in three Griffith features, *The Idol Dancer*, with Clarine Seymour and Richard Barthelmess, *Way Down East*, in which he played Professor Sterling, and *Orphans of the Storm*, with Lillian and Dorothy Gish. In the last, playing a lesser role of Picard, Creighton Hale demonstrated the fine character-playing of which he was capable.

During the twenties, Hale was much in demand as a featured player or leading man in films such as *Fascination* (1922), *Trilby* (1923), *The Marriage Circle* (1924), *Beverly of Graustark* (1926), and *Annie Laurie* (1927). One of Creighton Hale's last starring roles was as the seriocomic hero of *The Cat and the Canary*. As *Picture Show* commented, "He makes no attempt to appear impressive. He is just natural." This 1927 Universal feature, directed by the German Paul Leni and co-starring Laura La Plante, was later remade as a talkie with Bob Hope in the Creighton Hale role. The actor played a similar type of part in Benjamin Christensen's interesting, if flawed, *Seven Footprints to Satan* (1929).

In 1929, Hale met up again with House Peters, when the two played Etienne and Sergeant Terence Malone respectively in M-G-M's *Rose Marie*. A young Joan Crawford essayed the title role.

Creighton Hale continued making films with the coming of sound, appearing in numerous films in the thirties, few of which are worth recalling. He was one of a group of silent stars featured in a 1936 Paramount production, *Hollywood Boulevard*. In 1940, Hale became one of the many former silent stars under contract to Warner Bros., where his films included *The Bride Came C.O.D.*, *Crime by Night*, *Torchy Plays with Dynamite,* and *Bullet Scars*. In 1947, for old time's sake, he had a walk-on part in Paramount's shabby tribute to Pearl White, *The Perils of Pauline*. Creighton Hale's final years were spent at the Motion Picture Country House in Woodland Hills, California, and at an old actors' home in Pasadena, where he died on Monday, August 9, 1965.

"Moore is one of the permanent names in the early history of motion pictures," wrote Julian Johnson in 1917.[8] Unusual among the Moores were three brothers, Matt (1888–1960), Owen (1886–1939), and Tom (1885–1955), all of whom were actually born in Ireland—in County Meath. As Tom Moore recalled, in true romantic Irish fashion, their father turned over ownership of the family cottage to his wife's brother. The family then climbed aboard a jaunting car and:

> At the top of the little hill we paused and looked back. The little valley which had held our lives was full of bright sunshine. My father was happy on the edge of a great new adventure, we kids were as excited as he, and my mother, I remember, was crying a little. Father wore a tall hat, which he took off and put down on the seat of the car. Taking a pencil he tore an envelope into strips, wrote a name upon each strip, and put them all into the hat. The names were "America," "The Continent," "London," "South America," "The Orient," and so forth. He looked over the six children until he came to Joe, who was a tiny baby then. Whispering to Joe he held the hat in front of him, shaking it temptingly. If Joe had any thoughts he probably suspected it held something good to eat, for in went his hand, and when it came out he held, all crumpled up, the slip on which was written "America." Joe had made the decision. A week later we sailed for New York.[9]

With distinctive features and fairly heavily built, the Moore brothers were not typical screen leading men, and yet each enjoyed reasonable success during the silent era. Owen entered films first, circa 1908, followed by Tom four years later, and Matt a year after that. Owen became the biggest star, marrying Mary Pickford in 1910—they were divorced in 1920—and playing opposite her in a number of films from the early 'teens. Tom also married an actress; in fact, two of them, first Alice Joyce and later Renée Adorée. The three brothers were co-starred in the 1929 feature *Side Street*. With the coming of sound, the Moore boys continued their careers as character players, and each remained active until his death.

The only other Irish-born actor to star in silent films was William Desmond (1878–1949), who came to New York, as a child, from his native Dublin. After many years on the stage, he made his screen debut opposite Billie Burke in *Peggy* (1915). Like the Moore brothers, Desmond was a well-built leading man, who quickly became stereotyped as a leading man or supporting player in Westerns, serials, and other action pictures. Although the importance of the roles diminished, Desmond remained active almost until the end of his life, billing himself in later years as "the veteran of a thousand films."

Although their films might have international appeal, there are some Irishmen, such as actors Max Adrian (born 1903 in Enniskillen, Northern

Ireland), Eddie Byrne (born 1911 in Dublin), Cyril Cusack (born 1910 in Durban, South Africa, but raised in Ireland), and director Montgomery Tully (born 1904 in Dublin), whose work on screen has largely been limited to Europe. Joyce Redman (born 1918 in County Mayo) has twice received Academy Award nominations for Best Actress—for her work in *Tom Jones* (1963) and *Othello* (1965)—but she has yet to work in Hollywood.

She never became the major star that she deserved to be, but Maureen O'Hara is, arguably, the best known of Irish-born Hollywood actresses, having first seen the light of day in Millwall, near Dublin, on August 17, 1920. With her green eyes and flaming red hair, she looked simply stunning in such Technicolor epics of the forties as *The Spanish Main* (1945) and *Sinbad the Sailor* (1947). However, she had commenced her screen career in more demure, quieter roles, making a lasting impression in *Dance Girl Dance* (1940) and *How Green Was My Valley* (1941). As *Look* (November 20, 1951) pointed out, she "blossomed from a timid colleen into the queen of the slashing sword and the flying fist," and she displayed a goodly amount of the latter in John Ford's *The Quiet Man* (1952).

Born Maureen FitzSimmons, the actress adopted the name O'Hara with the commencement of her film career, which had its origins in her training with the Abbey Theatre School and small roles on the Abbey stage. She came to London, and American entertainer Harry Richman arranged a screen test for her; a couple of minor film roles followed, and then she was cast by Charles Laughton as the heroine of *Jamaica Inn* (1939). O'Hara also played with Laughton in *The Hunchback of Notre Dame* (1939) and *This Land Is Mine* (1943). Maureen O'Hara has not been seen on screen since the seventies, as she has become a businesswoman involved in publishing and running a small airline. Her presence is missed.

Born on May 17, 1911, in County Roscommon, Maureen O'Sullivan was discovered, as already noted, during the filming of location scenes for *Song o' My Heart*. Her best known role was that of Jane in a series of Tarzan films: *Tarzan the Ape Man* (1932), *Tarzan and His Mate* (1934), *Tarzan Escapes* (1936), *Tarzan Finds a Son* (1939), and *Tarzan's New York Adventure* (1942). She was also memorable in *The Barretts of Wimpole Street* (1934), *David Copperfield* (1935), and *A Yank at Oxford* (1938). With her almost prim English accent and her rosy-cheeked English schoolgirl complexion, only her name gave away Maureen O'Sullivan's Irish origins.

There was no mistaking the origins of George Brent (1904–1979), who was born George Nolan in Shannonbridge and was actively involved with the Irish Republican Army in the 'teens, so much so that he eventually began billing himself as "a fighting Irishman." His activities in the Irish Rebellion led to Brent's having to escape the country, and, finally, he settled in the United States. In Hollywood, Brent became a competent leading man who could be relied upon not to detract from the allure of leading ladies like Bette Davis, Greta Garbo, Ginger Rogers, and Olivia de Havilland.

Maureen O'Hara

Dan O'Herlihy was born in Wexford on May 1, 1919, and gained stage experience at both the Abbey and Gate Theatres, as well as working as an announcer for Radio Éireann, before making his screen debut in *Hungry Hill* (1946). He was featured by Carol Reed as Nolan in *Odd Man Out* (1947) and then came to the United States, where he worked with Orson Welles, playing Macduff in Welles' 1947 stage version and 1948 screen version of Shakespeare's *Macbeth*. O'Herlihy obviously appealed to directors of a higher intellectual order, as evidenced by his being cast in the title role of the Mexican production of *The Adventures of Robinson Crusoe* (1952) by Luis Buñuel. (He was nominated for an Academy Award for his performance.) Dan O'Herlihy continues to act, albeit occasionally, on screen and has been featured in three

American television series, *The Travels of Jaimie McPheeters* (ABC, 1963-1964), *The Long, Hot Summer* (ABC, 1965-1966), and *A Man Called Sloane* (NBC, 1979-1980). In passing, it might be noted that O'Herlihy has portrayed two American presidents: John F. Kennedy in the 1972 Abbey Theatre production of *The White House* and Franklin D. Roosevelt in Universal's 1977 production of *MacArthur*.

Born Kieron O'Hanrahan in Skibbereen in 1925, Kieron Moore has appeared in both British and American films since 1945. He is one of those handsome, easygoing actors who seems to make little impression on the viewer, and yet his list of films is impressive, including *Anna Karenina* (1948), in which he played Count Vronsky opposite Vivien Leigh, and *Darby O'Gill and the Little People*, in which he appeared as Pony Sugrue. The latter was based on stories by H.T. Kavanagh, which Walt Disney had first considered filming in the forties. Disney made a trip to Ireland in 1948, and at that time announced plans for the film, then to be called *The Little People*. Despite the presence of such Irish actors as Jimmy O'Dea, Denis O'Dea and Jack MacGowran, the film was actually shot in California, with special effects artist Peter Ellenshaw providing paintings of Irish backgrounds for use in matte shots.

Richard Harris began his screen career with two films with Irish themes, *Shake Hands with the Devil* (1959) and *A Terrible Beauty* (1960), which was released in the United States as *The Night Fighters*. He was born on October 1, 1932, in Limerick, and gained an international reputation with his performance in *This Sporting Life* (1963). His screen image is one of roughness, unbroken by any redeeming features, but with his starring opposite Vanessa Redgrave in the 1967 screen version of the musical *Camelot* his characterizations seem to have softened, and he has returned to the stage (where his career began in 1956) to tour both the United Kingdom and the United States as Camelot's fabled King Arthur.

As Richard Harris has calmed down through the years, his countryman Peter O'Toole has become more eccentric in his characterizations. Born in Connemara on October 2, 1932, O'Toole was educated in England and made his stage debut at the age of 17 with the Leeds Civic Theatre. He has been a major star from the sixties onwards, with his films including *Lawrence of Arabia* (1962), *Beckett* (1964), *The Lion in Winter* (1968), *The Ruling Class* (1972), and *The Stuntman* (1978). O'Toole was particularly memorable in Hugh Leonard's seven-part adaptation of James Plunkett's novel *Strumpet City*, produced by RTÉ in 1980.

Milo O'Shea (who was born in Dublin on June 2, 1926) will probably be remembered in years to come more as a stage actor than a screen performer, despite his starring role in the 1967 film version of *Ulysses*. He first came to the United States in 1951 as a member of the Dublin Players, but he was not featured in a Broadway production until *Staircase* in 1968. He toured in the major American revival of *My Fair Lady* in 1979, essaying the role of Alfred P. Doolittle, and the following year enjoyed his greatest stage success as Father

Tim Farley in Bill C. Davis' play *Mass Appeal*. O'Shea's film career began in 1951 with an uncredited role as a sign writer in *Talk of a Million*, released in the United States as *You Can't Beat the Irish*. The films in which he did receive billing are generally unmemorable: *Never Put It in Writing* (1964), *Romeo and Juliet* (1968), *Paddy* (1970), and *Percy's Progress* (1974, and released in the United States as *It's Not the Size That Counts*), among others.

Pierce Brosnan is the biggest and best-looking international star to emerge from Ireland in recent years. Born in Navan, County Meath, Brosnan makes little mention of his Irish background, despite his first major break as an actor coming with his being cast as Rory O'Manion in the 1981 miniseries, aired on ABC television, *The Manions of America*. Brosnan told *Ladies' Home Journal* (January 1985) that the series was "six hours of Irish tragedy in which I cried over my dead mother, then cried over my dead brother, and finally cried over my dead horse." The actor is best known on television for his starring in the title role on *Remington Steele*, which was seen on NBC from 1982 through 1986.

The actor made his screen debut in a very minor role, as a homosexual character, in the 1982 British feature *The Long Good Friday*. He made his American feature film debut in a 1986 production titled *Nomads*, which was badly received by both the public and the critics—J. Hoberman in *The Village Voice* (March 11, 1986) called it "self-confidently awful." Brosnan almost landed the role of James Bond in the film series loosely based on Ian Fleming's books, but at the last moment the role was given to Timothy Dalton, who replaced an aging Roger Moore.

It is worth noting that one of the James Bond films, *Thunderball*, released in 1965 by United Artists, was produced by Irish-born Kevin McClory. McClory had been associated with Mike Todd on the 1956 production of *Around the World in 80 Days*, and also worked with John Huston on *The African Queen*, *Moulin Rouge*, *Beat the Devil*, and *Moby Dick*. He produced, directed and co-wrote an interesting and little known 1959 British feature, *The Boy and the Bridge*.

There is one American screenwriter who deserves recognition in this chapter, and he is Benjamin Glazer (1887–1956), who was born in Belfast and came to the United States with his family, settling in Philadelphia, at the age of four. Glazer was active in the theatre, adapting Ferenc Molnar's *Liliom* for the American stage and served in the twenties as head of the story department at Paramount. In 1927, he received the first Academy Award for Best Writing—Adaptation for his work on *7th Heaven*, thus making him the first Irishman to win an Oscar. (He received a second Academy Award in 1940 for *Arise My Love*.)

Among Glazer's other film writing credits are *The Merry Widow* (1925), *Flesh and the Devil* (1927), *Mata Hari* (1932), *A Farewell to Arms* (1933), and *We're Not Dressing* (1934). He later turned to production and also wrote and directed *Song of My Heart* in 1948.

One may tend to assume that the Irish theatre revolves around the Abbey and the Gate, both in Dublin, but Ulster also has a twentieth century theatrical tradition, with the Ulster Literary Theatre, the Belfast Repertory Theatre Company (at the Empire Theatre), the Ulster Group Theatre, the Belfast Arts Theatre, and the Lyric Players Theatre. It is not surprising, therefore, that Northern Ireland should have provided its fair share of screen stars.

Born in County Down on September 29, 1908, Greer Garson is the most "English" of Irish ladies, thanks to her prim, sometimes wooden performances in such films as *Goodbye, Mr. Chips* (1939), *Pride and Prejudice* (1940), *Mrs. Miniver* (1942), and *Random Harvest* (1942). Equally English is Valerie Hobson, born in Larne, on April 14, 1917. She made a few American films in 1935 (most notably *The Bride of Frankenstein*), but the bulk of her career was in England, where her credits include *Great Expectations* (1946), *Kind Hearts and Coronets* (1949), and *The Rocking Horse Winner* (1949). Her film career ended when she married her second husband, John Profumo, a British Cabinet minister who was involved in the 1963 sex scandal concerning Christine Keeler and others. In direct opposite to Garson and Hobson is Siobhán McKenna, born in Belfast on May 24, 1923, who is decidedly Irish in films such as *Hungry Hill* (1946) and *The Playboy of the Western World* (1962). If God is an Englishman, then there is little reason why his son's earthly mother should not have been Irish, and thus McKenna was cast as the Virgin Mary in the 1961 production of *The King of Kings*. However, Siobhán McKenna's films have been few, and she is primarily a stage actress, having first come to prominence with the Abbey Theatre. She died on November 16, 1986.

Brian Donlevy (1899-1972) was born in Portadown, County Armagh, but left Ireland at the age of ten months when his father emigrated to the United States. He gained a reputation in Hollywood for tough, sadistic roles, such as the sergeant in *Beau Geste* (1939), for which he was nominated for an Academy Award, but one should not ignore his fine comedic performance in Preston Sturges' 1941 production of *The Great McGinty* and 1944 production of *The Miracle at Morgan's Creek*. Born in Belfast on July 4, 1928, Stephen Boyd began his career in Canada and enjoyed his biggest success as Messala in the 1959 production of *Ben-Hur*. This led to typecasting, with his later films including *The Fall of the Roman Empire* (1964) and *The Bible* (1966).

Colin Blakely, born in Bangor on September 23, 1930, is a fine, stockily built actor, whose film career has been limited to the United Kingdom. Among his best films are *Saturday Night and Sunday Morning* (1960), *This Sporting Life* (1963), and *The Private Life of Sherlock Holmes* (1970). Along with Joyce Redman, he was the only Irish actor to be cast in Laurence Olivier's National Theatre production of *Juno and the Paycock*. In an interview a few years ago, he commented, "I think of myself as an Irishman but not as an Ulsterman.... A year ago I had thought of looking for a house in Northern Ireland; today I have decided to find a house in the Republic. I would rather live in Ireland than die in Ireland."[10] He died on May 7, 1987.

Where Irish players have excelled themselves in Hollywood productions is as character actors and actresses. Without the benefit of stardom, without their names above the titles, Barry Fitzgerald, Arthur Shields, Una O'Connor, J.M. Kerrigan, Sara Allgood, and others have added immeasurably to the films in which they appeared.

The greatest of all the Irish character actors and, arguably, the greatest of all Irish stage actresses of this century is Sara Allgood. Micheál Mac Liammóir wrote of her work in the theatre, "As it is impossible to describe acting of this calibre, I will point to the real tragedy of Cathleen Ni Houlihan [Mother Ireland] in being unable to hold such children close to her forever."[11] It is a tragedy that Sara Allgood should have spent such a comparatively small amount of time performing in Ireland, but, at the same time, it is a blessing that she made so many films first in the United Kingdom and then the United States, even if many of those films fail to do justice to her art.

Born into a working-class Dublin family on October 31, 1893, Sally Allgood, as she was affectionately known, was educated at the Marlborough Street Training College. In the early years of this century, she joined the Irish National Theatre Society (run by William Fay, and later to merge with Yeats' and Lady Gregory's Irish Literary Theatre and become the Abbey Theatre). In 1903, she had a small speaking part in W.B. Yeats' *The King of Threshold*, and it is said that after her performance, the poet turned to Fay and said, "You have an actress there."

Sara Allgood made her first film appearance in 1918 while touring Australia with her husband Gerald Henson in the play *Peg o' My Heart*. The film was *Just Peggy*, directed by Joe Lipman for Mia Films. A reporter in the *Sydney Daily Telegraph* wrote, "Sara, for a salary of 100 pounds a week for six weeks, spent her free time on an open air movie stage on the heights above Middle Harbor. Here puckering her brow against the Australian sun, she starred in *Just Peggy*, a drama of two generations, involving a runaway child." On her first screen appearance, Allgood commented, "It seemed to me, while peeping at the silent camera perched on its tripod, that from the lens aperture the whole world was looking at me. My first day in front of a camera was a far worse ordeal than any first night could ever be."

Her next film appearance was not until 1929 and Alfred Hitchcock's first talkie, *Blackmail*, in which she had a small role as Anny Ondra's mother, with less than a dozen words to speak. The following year, Hitchcock began filming Sean O'Casey's *Juno and the Paycock*, with Sara Allgood in the role she had first created at the Abbey in 1924 and on the London stage in 1925. Of her speaking of Juno's final prayer, W.B. Yeats had said that it transcended folk art and the Dublin slums and even Ireland.

Eileen Crowe recalled for me that her husband, F.J. McCormick, took Hitchcock all over Dublin to show him the reality which the play attempted to transfer to the stage. Unfortunately, Hitchcock was too much of a filmmaker to leave O'Casey's play intact. Juno's soliloquy is destroyed by the director's continually cutting away from Sara Allgood's face to one object or another and by the introduction of sickly sweet background music. He cast Edward Chapman rather than Barry Fitzgerald as Captain Boyle. So displeased with the film was Sean O'Casey that he would not permit its screening during his lifetime.

Throughout the thirties, Sara Allgood continued to appear in British films, including *The Passing of the Third Floor Back* (1936), *It's Love Again* (1936), *Kathleen Mavourneen* (1937), and *Storm in a Teacup* (1937). In 1940, she came to New York to appear on Broadway in *Juno and the Paycock*, and decided to try her luck in Hollywood, where she was to spend the remainder of her life, becoming an American citizen in 1945.

One of her first Hollywood films, *How Green Was My Valley* (1941), was her best, with her performance as the mother dominating the film. Unhappily, Sara Allgood's later career in Hollywood did not live up to her earlier expectations. Her niece, Mrs. Pauline Hague, recalled,

> Sally went to Hollywood with high hopes. Being the great artist she was it was a shock to her, to say the least, to be treated in a high-handed manner. I'll never forget one thing she said to me when I was in her beautiful Spanish home in Beverly Hills. She hadn't been getting much work and Mr. Bernie (her agent) was urging her to give a big party and invite important people to it. Sally was dreadfully depressed and later said to me, "I could never do a thing like that. I could never prostitute my art." Another thing she said, "When you go back to your home and your family you can think of me sitting alone—afraid to go out for fear I should miss a call to work." This was sheer tragedy.[12]

Small parts did, however, come Sara Allgood's way, usually in 20th Century–Fox productions. Occasionally she did get an opportunity to shine, as in *It Happened in Flatbush* (1942), in which she plays an eccentric lady running the Brooklyn baseball club, or Ernst Lubitsch's *Cluny Brown* (1946), in which she appears as the protocol-bound head servant of Reginald Owen's estate. Her last film was *Cheaper by the Dozen* (1950); "The salary is cut to the bone but no matter, it's activity, and that's the main thing," she wrote to Gabriel Fallon.

Sara Allgood died in Hollywood, following a heart attack on September 3, 1950. She left an estate valued at $50,000. Two years later, on November 2, 1952, her sister, Máire O'Neill, was burnt to death after falling in a fire in an alcoholic stupor.

Although not as well remembered as her sister, Máire O'Neill had also been a prominent member of the Abbey Theatre Company. Irish theatre historian Micheál Ó hAodha has written that "the names of Sara Allgood and her sister Máire O'Neill sum up the chief virtues of the Abbey style of acting."[13] She was a busy character actress in British films of the thirties and forties, memorable as Madame Osiris in the Gracie Fields vehicle *Sing as We Go*

Sara Allgood and John Laurie in *Juno and the Paycock*.

(1934). Eileen Crowe remembers that she had a caustic tongue, and while Eileen was appearing in *Hungry Hill*, Máire O'Neill came on the set. At the end of the scene, O'Neill remarked in the most devastating of tones, "So *this* is Eileen Crowe."

Eileen Crowe (1899–1978) was primarily a good actress, the best at the Abbey after the departure of Sara Allgood. She made only a few films: *The Plough and the Stars* (1936), *Hungry Hill* (1947), *Top o' the Morning* (1949), *The Quiet Man* (1952), *The Rising of the Moon* (1957), *A Terrible Beauty/The Night Fighters* (1960), *Home Is the Hero* (1961), and *Girl with Green Eyes* (1964). In 1925, she married Peter Judge, who appeared at the Abbey Theatre under the name of F.J. McCormick (1891–1947). He was regarded as the most

Barry Fitzgerald

versatile of Irish actors, born in Skerries, and of his Joxer in *Juno and the Paycock*, Sean O'Casey said he had created a comic figure even greater than the dramatist's concept of the part. F.J. McCormick appeared in only three features: *The Plough and the Stars* (1936), *Hungry Hill* (1947) and *Odd Man Out* (1947).

Also from the Abbey Theatre came J.M. Kerrigan (1887–1964), who was born in Dublin, and appeared in countless American films from the mid twenties through the late fifties. He was always typecast as an "Irish" character.

Probably the best known of male Irish character performers is Barry Fitzgerald (1888–1961), who was born William Joseph Shields in Dublin. After appearances in a couple of British films—*Juno and the Paycock* (1930) and

When Knights Were Bold (1936)—he came to the United States for *The Plough and the Stars* in 1937, and stayed, to appear in more than 30 features, in many of which he portrayed very irritating Irish characters with heavy brogues. His best known role, for which he won an Academy Award for Best Supporting Actor, is that of Father Fitzgibbon in *Going My Way* (1944). There was a certain sameness to Fitzgerald's performances, even when he was playing villains, and it is a little difficult to determine if he was actually a good actor who could not overcome his film material or he was simply mediocre.

Although not as well known as his brother, Arthur Shields (1896–1970) was probably a better actor. He was also a graduate of the Abbey Theatre, where he gained the nickname of "Boss," and was well liked by John Ford at least until *The Quiet Man* (1952), when the director turned against him. Shields was always typecast as an "Irish" character, and among his best films are *The Plough and the Stars* (1936), *Drums Along the Mohawk* (1939), *How Green Was My Valley* (1941), and *She Wore a Yellow Ribbon* (1949).

One Irish character actress who could always be relied upon to entertain in her roles was Una O'Connor (1880–1959), who came to Hollywood in 1932, when Noel Coward insisted she should recreate her stage role of the sorrowful maid, Ellen Bridges, in the screen adaptation of his *Cavalcade*. She had already appeared in at least four British films (from 1929) and was to appear in more than 50 American ones. She was, of course, good in *The Informer* (1935) and *The Plough and the Stars* (1936), but one remembers Una O'Connor best for her curious, rolling walk in *The Barretts of Wimpole Street* (1934) and for her piercing screams in *The Invisible Man* (1933) and *Bride of Frankenstein* (1935). Unlike her fellow Irish character players, she could just as easily be cast as an "English" eccentric than as an "Irish" one.

Why do Irish players appeal to American producers? The answer lies, this author believes, in a comment made by James Agate in his review of the film version of *The Plough and the Stars*: "They are all of them mighty phrasemakers; they are soil for the most grandiose flowers of speech. Yet what a lot they are if we stop to consider them dispassionately!"[14] What a wonderful, entertaining lot indeed.

V. The Irish Image on American Screens

Reviewing the IMP Company production of *Kathleen Mavourneen*, George Blaisdell commented in *The Moving Picture World* (March 18, 1913) that the "picture will appeal to all of Irish blood — which means that it will have universal appeal; for Irish plays, like Irish songs, reach every heart." It was a philosophy which the American film industry embraced wholeheartedly, particularly during the silent era, and to a lesser extent with the coming of sound; films with Irish themes were a regular feature at America's movie theatres. The setting was Ireland and the subject was either romance or patriotism — two topics which could not fail to arouse any audience.

It is impossible to document just how many films with Irish themes have been produced by the American film industry, just as it is impossible to determine which was the first such production. Between 1908 and 1920, more than a dozen American films were released beginning with the words "Ireland" or "Irish." Typical of pre-1910 productions with Irish themes is Selig's one-reel release from October 1, 1908, titled *A Daughter of Erin*. A poor Irish colleen marries a gentleman above her station; he attempts to have her killed, but she is rescued by her childhood sweetheart, a village lad named Miles. According to contemporary publicity, the highlight of the production was "as pretty a six-handed Irish fight as one could wish to see." Another Selig production, released in January 1908, was *The Irish Blacksmith*, which was advertised as "Romantic Irish Drama of the typical kind."

Kathleen Mavourneen, whose title character is abducted by a villainous, rich landlord almost from the arms of her lover, Terence O'More, was first filmed by the Edison Company in 1906. The most important screen version came in 1913 and was directed by Irishman Herbert Brenon for the IMP Company. It featured Jane Fearnley as Kathleen and William Shay as Terence O'More, supported by Frank Smith, William Welch, Robert Ferguson, and Fred Turner. "Mr. Brenon has builded carefully and well," reported George Blaisdell in *The Moving Picture World* (March 8, 1913). "For a foundation he created atmosphere. In his first scene it was noticeable. It was the interior of an Irish cabin. In his second it was marked. A bit of lane, with the lowroofed

Charles Rogers and Nancy Carroll in *Abie's Irish Rose*.

white buildings, mentally removes you to a little Irish village. And there you remain until the end of the play. It is a picture that will hold an audience — and send it home in a happy frame of mind."

Presumably because both groups represented major portions of the filmgoing audience, the interrelationship between Irish-Americans and Jewish-Americans has held a particular interest for filmmakers. As early as March 20, 1910, Champion released a one-reel production titled *Ireland and Israel*, which dealt with the friendship between Pat Riley, an Irish inhabitant of the Battery, and Abie Wedetzky, a newly arrived immigrant. Abie prospers, after changing his name, and is able to help Pat in his time of need.

From the night it opened at the Fulton Theatre, New York, on May 23,

1922, Anne Nichols' *Abie's Irish Rose* became one of the most popular of stage productions. It ran for 2,327 performances. In his original review in *Life* (June 8, 1922), Robert Benchley wrote, *"The Rotters* is no longer the worst play in town! *Abie's Irish Rose* has just opened!" Benchley lived to regret his dismissal of the play, and each year was to publish a new, equally negative, review, at one point arguing with Miss Nichols that the play was not, as she suggested, a preachment for tolerance and brotherly love, but rather it teemed with racial hatred and intolerance.

Abie's Irish Rose was the story of Abie Levy who meets and falls in love with Rosemary Murphy. He introduces her to his family as Rosie Murpheski, and the two are married by a rabbi, only to be remarried, upon the arrival of Mr. Murphy, by a priest. The two families are appeased on Christmas Eve when introduced to Abie and Rosemary's twin children, one of whom is named Patrick Joseph (after Rosemary's father) and the other Rebecca (after Abie's dead mother).

The play was too successful not to be filmed, and, in 1929, Paramount released the screen version, directed by Victor Fleming, and starring Charles Rogers (as Abie), Nancy Carroll (as Rosemary), Jean Hersholt (as Abie's father), and J. Farrell MacDonald (as Rosemary's father). "What the film theatre gets from *Abie* is the commercial advantage of the best publicized title in the world," commented *Variety* (April 25, 1928). "The play material itself is a handicap. Hollywood could turn out funnier comedies on the same subject."

Anne Nichols wrote the screenplay for a new version of her play, produced by Bing Crosby, and released in the fall of 1946 by United Artists. The second screen adaptation was directed by A. Edward Sutherland, and starred Joanne Dru (as Rosemary), Richard Norris (as Abie), Michael Chekhov (as Abie's father), and J.M. Kerrigan (as Rosemary's father). The new version starts on V-E Day in London as Abie meets USO camp show entertainer Rosemary, and the couple are married there by a Protestant army chaplain. However, times had changed, and many in the audience were offended by Michael Chekhov's Jewish stereotype.

In 1927, Robertson-Cole produced a feature titled *Clancy's Kosher Wedding*, directed by Arvid E. Gillstrom, and featuring George Sidney and Will Armstrong. It bore a slight similarity to *Abie's Irish Rose*, and an even closer similarity to a group of films which were to be released by Universal in the years ahead, chronicling the adventures of the Cohens and the Kellys. In 1925, Aaron Hoffman had written a play titled *Two Blocks Away*, about a Jewish drygoods store-owner named Jacob Cohen and a New York cop named Patrick Kelly, who were always arguing with each other, particularly over Cohen's daughter, Nannie, and Kelly's son, Tim. Eventually, it is discovered that a fortune inherited by Cohen is rightfully Kelly's, and the two men, reconciled, go into business together. Universal released a film version of the play in 1926 under the title of *The Cohens and the Kellys*. Harry Pollard was the director, and George Sidney was featured as Cohen, Charlie Murray as Kelly, Vera Gordon as Mrs. Cohen, and Kate Price as Mrs. Kelly.

The film gave birth to a series, which had the Cohens and Kellys as partners in a business which changed from feature to feature. Six subsequent films were released: *The Cohens and Kellys in Paris* (1928), *The Cohens and Kellys in Atlantic City* (1929), *The Cohens and Kellys in Scotland* (1930), *The Cohens and Kellys in Africa* (1930), *The Cohens and Kellys in Hollywood* (1932), and *The Cohens and Kellys in Trouble* (1933). George Sidney was featured in all six sequels; Vera Gordon and Kate Price were featured in the first four; Charlie Murray was seen in all but *The Cohens and Kellys in Paris* and *The Cohens and Kellys in Atlantic City*, in which he was replaced, respectively, by J. Farrell MacDonald and Mack Swain. Popular with the general film audience in the twenties, the series seemed remarkably dated in the thirties, and Universal was well advised to end it in 1933.

Other features from the twenties which dealt with the interrelationship between the Irish and the Jews in New York include *Kosher Kitty Kelly* (1926), *A Harp in Hock* (1927) and *The Shamrock and the Rose* (1927).

To return to the 'teens years, the success of the Kalem films shot in Ireland led other American companies to release films with Irish backgrounds, but filmed in the United States. Among these were the IMP Company's *Shamus O'Brien*, a two-reel drama, released in Ireland on May 12, 1912. Featuring King Baggott in the title role, the production was a faithful picturization of Samuel Lover's poem, and, as *The Bioscope* pointed out, "Whether Irish or not, it gives one the Irish impression." From the Philadelphia-based Lubin Company came *An Irish Girl's Love*, a one-reel romance released in Ireland on January 5, 1913. The Domino Company was responsible for *Eiline of Erin*, one reel in length and released in Ireland on April 23, 1914, which it described as "a tale of rebellion in Ireland, and the manner in which the reverend father helps the women and children of Dennis, who is sentenced to death."

Also in 1914, Domino released *For the Wearing of the Green*. It was distributed in the United Kingdom and Ireland by the Award Film Service, which published a full-page advertisement for the production in the July 9, 1914, edition of *The Bioscope*, headed "Home Rule for Ireland." The advertisement continues, "*The Wearing of the Green* shows you in well illustrated form the suppression of Ireland in the early Victorian era, the plot also has running through it a very well thought out love story, which cannot help but hold your audience in gasps." Surprisingly, the British *Bioscope* was quite enthusiastic about the film. On July 2, 1914, it commented, "It is a picture which will enchant every Englishman, and turn every Irishman who sees it positively dizzy with enthusiasm. It is a magnificent Irish drama, full of fiery excitement and typically Celtic romanticism as regards its story, and exquisitely lovely as regards its setting."

In the summer of 1915 a new company was formed with the proud boast that everyone connected with it "from the office boy up to the president" was

Irish. The All-Celtic Company was to produce a series of "The Adventures of Peaceful Rafferty," directed by Charlie O'Hara, written by Pat Foy, and featuring Joe Sullivan, Peggy Shannon, Tom O'Keefe, Tommy Mullins, Tammany Young, Frank P. O'Donovan, and J.A. Fitzgerald. Each of the films, one reel in length, was released by the World Film Corporation, commencing with *Rafferty Settles the War*. At least two other films, *Rafferty Goes to Coney Island* and *Rafferty at the Hotel De Rest*, were filmed by the All-Celtic Film Company.

When Gene Gauntier and her husband, Jack Clark, joined Universal in 1915, their first film—released under the Bison 101 brand name—was *The Smuggler's Lass*, a two-reel "Irish Sea Coast Drama." Although shot in California, Universal advertised that "the scenes of the play are Irish with all the true Irish beauty and charm pictured faithfully." John Ford's brother, Francis, directed and co-starred with Grace Cunard in two Universal films with Irish themes. *The Cry of Erin*, released in March 1916, was based on the ballad "Shamus O'Brien." It was a typical Irish story of the hero escaping from the English gallows with the help of his girlfriend and the village priest. "Familiar in plot, but strong in action and atmosphere," reported *The Moving Picture World* (March 18, 1916). *Brennon o' the Moor*, a two-reel drama released in September 1916, told of an Irish highwayman who is captured by the British but escapes to the United States. *The Moving Picture World* (September 9, 1916) called it "A typical subject of the kind." Another "Irish" film from this period, released by Universal, was the three-reel "Gold Seal" drama, *The Duchess* (1915), starring Cleo Madison and Joe King.

Irish dramas reached the peak of their popularity in the mid 'teens. On November 9, 1916, Paramount released the Pallas feature *A Son of Erin*, "a story of old Ireland and of a fine young Irishman's strivings to make his fortune in America," starring Dustin Farnum. Mae Marsh and Robert Harron were featured in the Fine Arts comedy-drama *The Marriage of Molly-O*, directed by Paul Powell, and released by Triangle in the summer of 1916. Another Triangle release from 1916 was the Thomas H. Ince production of *A Corner in Colleens*, directed by Charles Miller, and featuring Bessie Barriscale and Charles Ray. Rex Ingram's wife-to-be, Alice Terry, was seen in this film in a small role. In 1918, Triangle released *Irish Eyes*, directed by William Dowlan, and starring Pauline Stark and Joe King. In a highly chauvinist review, a critic for the British *Kinematograph Weekly* commented, "No man could give reasons for all that women do; and probably to most kinema-goers the actions of the heroine of *Irish Eyes* will seem incomprehensible; while the whole of the action will seem very unlike anything which really happens in England. Still, it may possibly be a true picture of Irish life—so far as it goes—because no Englishman can give good reasons for what Irishmen do."

From Famous Players-Lasky/Paramount came a five-reel feature titled *Little Lady Eileen* (1916), featuring one of the most popular stars of the period, Marguerite Clark, under the direction of J. Searle Dawley. Also from the same studio came *Castles for Two* (1917), starring Marie Doro and Elliott Dexter, under the direction of Frank Reicher, and *Molly Entangled* (1917), starring Vivian Martin, under the direction of Robert Thornby. There were at least two Metro films with Irish themes released during 1917: *Bridges Burned*, a Popular Plans and Players production, directed by Perry Vekroff and starring English-born Madame Olga Petrova, who also wrote the screenplay; and *Peggy, the Will o' the Wisp*, a Rolfe production, starring Mabel Taliaferro, and directed by Tod Browning.

Among the other "Irish" films produced in Los Angeles during the 'teens years were *Denny from Ireland*, a comedy-drama starring Shorty Hamilton and Ellen Terry (not the great British stage actress), released in May 1918, and *The Lord Loves the Irish*, a Robert Brunton production, released by W.W. Hodkinson in December 1919, and starring J. Warren Kerrigan, under the direction of Ernest C. Warde. Another version of *Kathleen Mavourneen* was released in 1919, this time by William Fox, and with the decade's best known sex symbol, Theda Bara, appearing in the title role, with her husband, Charles Brabin, directing.

At this period, the Vitagraph Company was one of the oldest of American producing organizations. It had been founded by three Englishmen, J. Stuart Blackton, Albert E. Smith and William "Pop" Rock, and yet it released more than its share of Irish-related subjects. In 1918, William P.S. Earle directed a series of comedy-dramas for the studio, all starring New York–born Gladys Leslie, and all set in Ireland. Among the films were *His Own People* and *The Little Runaway*.

William P.S. Earle was also the director of a five-reel drama, *Whom the Gods Destroy*, released by Vitagraph on December 18, 1916. The film, which was written by Cyrus Townsend Brady and J. Stuart Blackton, featured Alice Joyce, Harry Morey, Marc MacDermott, and Charles Kent, and was, quite obviously, loosely based on the activities of Sir Roger Casement, an Irish patriot hanged in 1916 for encouraging Germany to intervene in Ireland's fight for independence from the United Kingdom.[1]

Whom the Gods Destroy told of Sir Denis Esmond, an Irish patriot, and Leslie St. George Leigh, a British naval officer, who are friends, and both in love with Mary O'Neil. With the fomenting of the Irish rebellion, Esmond is arrested as a traitor for his conspiracies against England. Leigh, who has been blinded during a submarine attack in the North Sea, is at Castle O'Neil with Esmond at the time of his supposed treachery, and he tries to extricate his friend by explaining that Esmond had repented before the acts which point to his guilt. However, the latter is condemned to die, but, with his influence, Leigh is able to reach the King and request a pardon. At first the King is unwilling to act, but he thinks of his own son and what his death might mean to him, and Esmond is granted his freedom. Thinking that Mary loves the Irish patriot, Leigh attempts to arrange a match between the two, but Mary assures him that it is he whom she loves.

The film was well received by the critics. *Motion Picture Magazine* (March 1917) called it "a heroic play, well done in every particular." *Exhibitor's Trade Review* (December 16, 1916) commented, "The theme is timely.... To the Irish it is vivid, and to those of English descent any tale connected with the tragedy of the Sinn Fein revolt will be interesting. Vitagraph has chosen a neutral path in presenting this story by taking the attitude that while freedom of Ireland from English sovereignty may be a good thing, it is best accomplished by other means than violence at a time when Britain is facing a great crisis."

Irish-Americans were less impressed. They viewed the film as evidence of a close link between J. Stuart Blackton, who had earlier been responsible for *The Battle Cry of Peace* (1915), which advocated preparedness in the United States and the British government. Mayor James M. Curley of Boston attended a screening at the city's Beacon and Olympic theatres, and with the Boston Board of Censors considered a complaint by the Friends of Irish Freedom of Boston that the feature was "slanderous and degrading." Mayor Curley and the board decided that "no action was necessary" on the protest.

In New York, the police commissioner refused to listen to complaints from the Sons of Irish Freedom, maintaining that the film was "perfectly proper and in no wise unneutral." Walter W. Irwin, Vitagraph's general manager, issued a statement, which read,

> Our London office has just informed us that *Whom the Gods Destroy* cannot be released in England, where it is considered too pro-Irish to be shown to English audiences. So much for the foolish charge that the British government subsidized or caused its production. I defy anybody with sober judgment to find anything in this picture in any way offensive to the Irish nation. The production reflects two points of view. *Whom the Gods Destroy* portrays the viewpoint of the Irishman who considers himself downtrodden and his country under the yoke of England. On the other hand it also depicts the viewpoint of England in its present struggle and the view, reasonable or unreasonable, that all of its subjects should and must fight for England. In other words, *Whom the Gods Destroy* shows how it is possible for two people who have diametrically opposite points of view to feel truthfully that each other has the right point of view and that the other is wrong. *Whom the Gods Destroy* brings out the best that is in both people. It illustrates with dramatic clarity that, fundamentally, there is really no difference in the human nature of the Irish and the English. Both possess, as this picture shows, a vast store of goodness, faithfulness, sincerity, kindness of heart and loyalty to their own ideas. No sane or sensible man could see this picture and get from it anything detrimental to the Irish, their ideas or their ideals. Those who get anything else from *Whom the Gods Destroy* must obviously be considered as fanatics. The protests that have arisen from such misguided people have been the source of the utmost surprise to the officers of this company and to the authors of the story. It was farthest from the minds of Commodore J. Stuart Blackton and the Rev. Dr. Cyrus Townsend Brady, who wrote *Whom the Gods Destroy*, to offend the Irish nation or

to stultify the magnificent qualities of the Irish people, which make them beloved by all the world. Doctor Brady is himself an Irish descendant and an intense Irish sympathizer.[2]

Despite Vitagraph's protestations, the film continued to create controversy and rioting. On January 13, 1917, Edward Moore and William Patrick Nolan (a brother of the national secretary of the Friends of Irish Freedom) were able to create a small panic at the Luna Theatre in Brooklyn through the use of "stink pots" and a tirade against the film. They were arraigned in a Brooklyn court, but the magistrate, an Irish-American gentleman by the name of Walsh, discharged the defendants.

Eamon De Valera's work with the Sinn Fein movement was the subject of *For the Freedom of Ireland*, originally produced by the Capital Film Company in 1920 and subsequently acquired, and apparently revised in some way, by the Creation Film Company. Hal Reid, who had formerly been with the Vitagraph Company, supplied a screenplay, which was directed by Roy Sheldon. The cast featured Vincent Coleman, Lawrence Fisher and Robert Klugston.

For the Freedom of Ireland dealt with the subject of a young Irish-American who goes to Ireland to aid the Sinn Feiners, is sentenced to death, but escapes and returns to the United States to aid De Valera in his campaign for American support. As the following comment by Mary Kelly from *The Moving Picture World* (October 23, 1920) indicates, the film presented a fairly biased view of its subject:

> This feature is another illustration of the fact that the screen has eclipsed all other mediums in presenting up-to-date facts in a vivid, impressive style. As propaganda it is more successful than as drama, although it is not without dramatic appeal. With the exception of the love story, most of its situations have an historical rather than fictitious flavor.
> Ireland is shown as an oppressed, misunderstood nation. Her innate powers of self-government, the resourcefulness and courage of her sons, her dependency upon America for aid are set forth in an interesting story. Whether the cruelty of the government in Ireland has not been overdrawn, might be a question. At any rate, their pictured treatment of the aged and of women is something almost Hunnish. The spiritual strength and undying faith of the Irish nation, as typified in the leading characters, are set forth with fine effect.
> Owing to faults in the continuity some of the events are precipitous, with the result that there is a lack of smoothness in the drama. The subtitles, too, are weak. If they were less "preachy," the picture's message would be all the more compelling.
> The cast is strong. Vincent Coleman, as a typical young American of Irish birth, has all the rash impetuosity and imaginative facility that his role calls for. The uncultivated beauty of the outdoor settings is another point of interest.

For the Freedom of Ireland also ran into problems. It was given its Chicago premiere before an invitational audience of 2,000 Friends of Irish Freedom at Orchestra Hall. The Chicago Film Censor subsequently decided that a number of cuts were in order before a public exhibition might be given.

Interest in Ireland and the Irish increased for American film producers in the twenties. More than 80 films were released in which the Irish in the United States were central characters. Among the more important of this group were *The Top o' the Morning* (1922), based on the 1913 play by Anne Caldwell; *Sweet Rosie O'Grady* (1926), based on the song of the same name; *The Little Irish Girl* (1926), with Dolores Costello in the title role; *Colleen* (1927), starring Madge Bellamy; and *Smiling Irish Eyes* (1929), featuring Colleen Moore. Laurette Taylor starred in the title role of *Peg o' My Heart*, a 1922 feature based on the popular 1918 play by her husband, J. Hartley Manners. It seems possible that D.W. Griffith was interested in producing a film on Ireland's troubles; there is a letter, dated January 16, 1923, in his papers at the Museum of Modern Art in New York which details conditions in Ireland at that time. *Kathleen Mavourneen* was filmed yet again, this time in 1930 by the small, independent company Tiffany, with Sally O'Neil—a discovery of Irish-American director Marshall Neilan—in the title role.

A number of films also boasted Irish settings. In 1921, Marion Davies starred in the Cosmopolitan production of *The Bride's Play*, based on a novel by Donn Byrne. A year later, Pat O'Malley was featured in Vitagraph's production of *My Wild Irish Rose*, based on Dion Boucicault's play *The Shaughraun*. Constance Binney was the star of Paramount's 1921 production of *Bed and Board*, in which an American helps an Irish heiress to save the family estate. *The Supreme Passion* (1921) was based on Thomas Moore's "Believe Me If All Those Endearing Young Charms."

It was the Irish and the Scotch in New York, rather than the Irish and the Jews, who were the subjects of *McFadden's Flats*, a 1927 First National release, based on a novel from the last century titled *McFadden's Row of Flats*. McFadden, played by Charlie Murray, is helped in his plans to build a block of apartments by a Scotch barber named McTavish, played by Chester Conklin. Along the way, McFadden's daughter and McTavish's son (played by Edna Murphy and Larry Kent) fall in love. The film was remade by Paramount in 1935 as a starring vehicle for Andy Clyde and Walter C. Kelly, a well-known vaudeville comedian billed as "The Virginia Judge."

Similar in style to *McFadden's Flats* was *The Callahans and the Murphys*, released later in 1927, and starring Marie Dressler and Polly Moran under the direction of George Hill. *Variety* (July 13, 1927) called it, "A medley of hoke and slapstick raised to the level of brilliant character comedy by legitimate acting." Irish-Americans called it an insult to their heritage, and rioting broke out in August of 1927 at two New York theatres at which the film was screening, Loew's Victoria Theatre and Loew's Orpheum Theatre. M-G-M, the film's producer, hastily produced two priests, Reverend Thomas F. Rudden and

Reverend William J. Fahay, both of St. Joseph's Church, Bound Brook, New Jersey, to endorse the film and also issued a statement reading: "The picture was made from a widely read story by Kathleen Norris. During production it was supervised by a staunch Irishman, J. Edward Mannix. All eliminations suggested by a group of Irish leaders were made before the picture was ever presented on the screen. It was passed by a board of censors."[3]

Because of its director (John Ford), its star (Janet Gaynor) and its source (Donn Byrne), *Hangman's House*, released by William Fox in the spring of 1928, remains one of the most important "Irish" films produced in the United States in the twenties. It is also important in that it did not burlesque the Irish. It did not oversentimentalize. It handled its subject with restraint. *Hangman's House* was a melodrama without melodramatics. John Ford created a believable Irish atmosphere, which was pictorially appealing.

The reviews were generally favorable. One fairly negative one, by Robert Benchley in *Life* (January 6, 1927), is worth reprinting in its entirety because it is entertainingly Benchley, and because it shows up a basic problem in dealing with heavily Irish authors, such as Donn Byrne:

> On the program for *Hangman's House* appeared a quotation from Donn Byrne's novel which evidently had been a source of great inspiration to Willard Mack in making his dramatization. According to Mr. Byrne, whenever a wandering Irishman meets a countryman, be it in Shanghai or Berlin, he asks the following questions concerning that widely advertised Fragment of Heaven:
> "Tell me is the Three Rock Mountain as purple as ever? Are the three-year-olds as wonderful as ever, as they charge up the Curragh mile? Are there swans on the Liffey? Are the fields still green? Tell me does the Irish wind whisper gently among the Irish trees, or was it only a dream of exile?"
> In spite of the fact that we are half–Irish ourself, we would be unable to answer any of the above questions except in the most general terms. It would seem safe, however, to take a chance and say that there are still swans on the Liffey. And if the three-year-olds referred to are the blooded stock used in the steeplechase in Act 3 of *Hangman's House*, we should say that they are something just short of "wonderful" even charging along the old *Ben-Hur* treadmill.
> We have an idea, however, that by the time these trenchant items appear in print the answer to a supplementary question, "And is *Hangman's House* still running at the auld Forrest Theatre?" would be the Gaelic equivalent of "No!"

Song o' My Heart was the best Irish-American feature of 1930, but it was certainly not the only one. In *Part Time Wife*, directed by Leo McCarey and produced by William Fox, an Irish caddie (played by Tom Clifford) helps a businessman save his marriage. Vera Reynolds was cast as an Irish "taxi dancer" from the Bronx in *The Last Dance*, directed by Scott Pembroke and produced by Audible Pictures. The Irish-Jewish theme was still in evidence in *Around The Corner*, directed by Bert Glennon and produced by Columbia, which featured George Sidney as Kaplan the Jew and Charlie Murray as O'Grady the Irishman. In 1935, the "Irish Mafia" at Warner Bros. enjoyed themselves in *The Irish in Us*, directed by Lloyd Bacon. The film cast Mary Gordon as a typical screen image of the Irish-American mother, with three sons, played by James Cagney, Pat O'Brien and Frank McHugh. *Variety* (August 7, 1935) called it, "A hokum holiday with everything thrown in. Built strictly for laughs, it's in no danger of being included in the Academy awards but it's in for good returns in the nabes and those downtown spots whose audiences go for a robust laugh and are not too particular about literary or production values." The film also helped introduce Olivia de Havilland, cast in the unlikely role of the daughter of Irish-American J. Farrell MacDonald, to the filmgoing public.

Irish politics were responsible for two American releases of 1937. A year earlier, while on vacation in Nice, France, Sam Goldwyn was persuaded to produce a romantic drama dealing with the life of Michael Collins, who had been the leader of the Sinn Fein movement and organized guerrilla warfare against the British, and who, in so doing, had helped create the Irish Free State and also got himself assassinated in 1922. The fact that Collins was not only the most heroic figure in twentieth century Irish history, but also was distinguishably handsome, possibly had something to do with Goldwyn's agreeing to produce such a film.

Three writers, John Balderston, Rose Franken and William Brown Meloney, were assigned to the film, which began life as *Covenant with Death*, and was subsequently called *In Love and War* and *Love Under Fire*, before being released as *Beloved Enemy*. A young stage director, H.C. Potter, was given his first film directorial assignment on the production, and a cast of English and Irish players was headed by Brian Aherne, Merle Oberon, Henry Stephenson, and Donald Crisp. A considerable amount of rewriting of Irish history took place in that Michael Collins here became Dennis Riordan who falls in love with Lady Helen Drummond (Merle Oberon) who comes over to Ireland with her father (Henry Stephenson), an emissary of the British government. Lady Helen charmingly helps Riordan create the Irish constitution, but he is shot by his best friend (Jerome Cowan), who believes he has betrayed Ireland out of his love for her. Two endings were filmed and screened; one in which Riordan dies and the other in which he recovers. The former appears to be the version most seen. "Strenuously romantic, magnificently acted and produced," commented *Time* (January 4, 1937), "it contains numerous moments of honest cinematic intensity."

The screen is still awaiting a good biography of Michael Collins. In 1968, Kevin McClory announced plans for a film to be based on Frank O'Connor's biography, *The Big Fellow*, with Collins' sister, Johanna, acting as an advisor. The film was to be made at Ardmore Studios, in widescreen, by Branwell Film Productions, with Sean Kenny (the great Tipperary-born theatrical artist) as production designer, and Richard Harris as Collins. Unfortunately nothing came of the project.

Not to be outdone by Sam Goldwyn's *Beloved Enemy*, Metro-Goldwyn-Mayer decided to produce a film on the life of Charles Stewart Parnell (1846–1891), who represented Irish nationalists in the British parliament and was responsible for Gladstone's introducing the first Home Rule bill in 1886. M-G-M announced that Clark Gable was to portray Parnell and Joan Crawford to play his lady love, Kitty O'Shea. When the studio was informed that Parnell's best known feature was his beard, it hastily organized research to prove that between 1880 and 1885, the years during which the film takes place, Parnell sported a moustache only. Thus, Clark Gable was not required to cover his facial features. Joan Crawford mysteriously dropped out of the project, and she was replaced by Myrna Loy. A deathbed scene, in which Gable was to speak by telephone to Loy, was dropped after researchers pointed out to director John Stahl that telephones were not in use in England in 1890.

The John Van Druten and S.N. Behrman script concentrated on little-known, indeed undocumented, romantic aspects of Parnell's life. Despite the Gable dimples being unhidden by a beard, the critics were not impressed by the production. In the *New York Times* (June 4, 1939), Frank S. Nugent opined that the *Encyclopaedia Britannica* entry on Parnell was more exciting than this film. "*Parnell*, which opened yesterday at the Capitol," he wrote, "struck me as being a singularly pallid, tedious, and unconvincing drama." Critics were doubly disappointed in that the play upon which it was based, by Elsie T. Schauffler, had been produced on Broadway the previous year and was remembered with respect and admiration. Only the anonymous critic for *Life* (June 14, 1937) seemed well pleased with the film. It was picked as the magazine's Movie of the Week, and hailed as "soundly conceived, shrewdly directed and capably acted."

As if to prove that John Ford was not the only director with a highly romanticized view of Ireland, David Miller — who is not exactly noted for the quality of his work — directed *Top o' the Morning* in 1949 for Paramount. The title is sufficient indication of the type of production — the phrase, "Top o' the Morning," is unknown in Ireland except among tour guides in Killarney anxious to please the American tourists. Originally titled *Needle in a Haystack* and scheduled for filming in Ireland, *Top o' the Morning* is concerned with the theft of the Blarney stone and the efforts of the local constable, played by Barry Fitzgerald, and an American insurance agent, played by Bing Crosby, to recover it. Crosby sings a few Irish traditional airs, as well as new songs by Johnny Burke and James Van Heusen, and ends up with the girl in the form of Ann Blyth as an unlikely Irish colleen. *Top o' the Morning* is best remembered for the performance of Eileen Crowe, despite such a great actress being wasted in the minor role of a resident of Blarney township.

The historical romanticism of Ireland drew producer Ross Hunter there in 1954 to film *Captain Lightfoot*, based on a novel by W.R. Burnett. Douglas Sirk directed this Universal-International release, which starred Rock Hudson in the title role, supported by Jeff Morrow, Barbara Rush, Kathleen Ryan, and

Brian Aherne (holding bicycle) in *Beloved Enemy*.

Denis O'Dea. The film was shot entirely on location in the Republic, with major locations including Beauparc, Slane Castle and the Powerscourt Estate. According to the *New York Times* (August 1, 1954), *Captain Lightfoot* was the first film to be shot wholly in Ireland. Although such a statement is obviously false as far as Irish and British films are concerned, it might very well be true with regard to American-financed productions.

A very unusual Irish image was to be found in *The Search for Bridey Murphy*, released by Paramount in the fall of 1956, which was concerned with a Colorado housewife (played by Teresa Wright), who through hypnosis goes back through an earlier reincarnation to become a 1798 Irish resident. Louis Hayward played the hypnotist who helped Bridey Murphy discover her former existence in a film directed and adapted by Noel Langley from a best-selling book by Morey Bernstein. The producer assured the viewing public that the film was directed, photographed and edited in such a way that there was no danger of any spectator falling into a hypnotic sleep.

The Big Gamble (1961), directed by Richard Fleischer and starring Stephen Boyd and Juliette Greco, opens in Dublin, where an Irish seaman persuades his family to finance a trucking business on the African Gold Coast. American producer and director Andrew S. Stone filmed his 1964 comedy,

Clark Gable and Myrna Loy in *Parnell*.

Never Put It in Writing, on location in England and Ireland. Starring Pat Boone and Milo O'Shea — an unlikely combination — the film dealt with an insurance executive who has to retrieve a letter of resignation written in a moment of anger. Walt Disney's *The Fighting Prince of Donegal* (1966) dealt with a legendary Irish hero and was based on the book *Red Hugh, Prince of Donegal* by Robert T. Reilly. The film, which starred Peter McEnery, Susan Hampshire and Gordon Jackson, featured a number of Irish performers, including Donald McCann, Maurice Roeves, Maire NiGhrainne, Moire O'Neill, and Fidelma Murphy, and marked the feature-film debut for Irish-born director Michael O'Herlihy.

Irish-Americans were represented in a number of American features of the sixties by an eclectic group of actors: Ralph Richardson in *Long Day's Journey into Night* (1962), Lawrence Harvey in *The Ceremony* (1963), Tom Tryon in *The Cardinal* (1963), Tommy Steele in *The Happiest Millionaire* (1967), Donovan O'Donnell in *The Vixen* (1968), Brian Keith in *The McKenzie Break* (1970), and Richard Harris in *The Molly Maguires* (1970). The last was an interesting drama, directed by Martin Ritt, which dealt with a secret society of immigrant Irish coal miners in eastern Pennsylvania. The music score utilized traditional Irish songs.

The songs in *Finian's Rainbow* were far from traditional, being the work of E.Y. Harburg and Burton Lane. The show had opened on Broadway on January 10, 1947, and was not filmed until 1968, by director Francis Ford Coppola for Warner Bros.-Seven Arts. Fred Astaire, Petula Clark and Tommy Steele starred in this story of an Irish rascal who buries a pot of stolen leprechaun gold, believing that it will multiply because the land is close to Fort Knox. A leprechaun named Og must search for the gold or become mortal. At the story's close he does become an ordinary man, marries the mortal with whom he has fallen in love, and the gold becomes dross. *Finian's Rainbow* was far from being the first film to deal with leprechauns. One of the earliest was Universal's 1935 production of *Night Life of the Gods*, based on the novel by Thorne Smith.

Leslie Waller's adventure novel about a rumrunner during Prohibition who acts as an agent for the IRA, *Change in the Wind*, was filmed in 1972 by director J.G. Works as *Irish Whiskey Rebellion*. The film, which features William Devane, Anne Meara, Richard Mulligan, and David Groh, was poorly received by both critics and public alike. *Boxoffice* (December 11, 1972) described it as "poorly edited, slow-moving and inconsistent in its plot developments."

The last important American production to have an Irish theme is *The Outsider*, a first film by director Tony Luraschi, an American living in France, who made the film for Paramount, where his father, Luigi Luraschi, was an executive. This overlong 1979 feature is important because it is the first film by a major studio to deal with the troubles in Northern Ireland, although, of course, it was actually filmed in Dublin, rather than Belfast, for a budget of slightly less than $3,000,000. Starring Craig Wesson, Sterling Hayden, Patricia Quinn, Niall O'Brien, and T.P. McKenna, *The Outsider* is based on the novel *The Heritage of Michael Flaherty* by Colin Leinster. It is the story of an American veteran of the Vietnam War who comes from a wealthy Detroit, Irish-American family, and who is inspired to come to Northern Ireland to fight for the IRA after hearing of his grandfather's heroic stories. The American is eventually framed for murder and becomes a political public relations tool for both the IRA and the British forces, more valuable to both sides dead than alive.

Rejected by the London Film Festival, in part it seems because the film is anti IRA, *The Outsider* was subsequently screened at the Los Angeles

International Film Festival (Filmex) and opened as an arthouse attraction in both London and Dublin in the spring of 1980. The British critics applauded the film, with its most vociferous supporter being Alexander Walker, film critic of the London *Evening Standard*, who just happens to be a native of Northern Ireland and is generally considered to be a conservative figure.

What is perhaps most interesting about *The Outsider* is that it is anti-American as much as anti-IRA. Paramount had the active support of the Irish Republican government in the film's production, and in responding to comments by Americans on the film's point of view, Bob Callahan wrote, "It is all too confusing to try to explain to these friends the continuing propaganda war being waged by the Dublin government against Irish Northern Aid, Irish National Caucus, and any and all Irish American support organizations who have chosen to back the nationalist struggle in the North. In truth the 'message' of *The Outsider* is the same message we have been hearing from at least three successive Dublin administrations: most crudely put, the message is, 'unless you come over as tourists, with lots of fat Yankee dollars in your pocket, Yanks stay out of it; and, by all means, Noraid go broke'."[4]

To a large extent, *The Outsider* is recompense for the patronizing overglamorized Irish-American productions which preceded it. It offers an unhappy truth with regard to the relationship between the Irish and the Irish-Americans. Ireland is an independent nation with its own, often confusing, political beliefs. All is not as black-and-white or as simple and innocent as American filmmakers would like the world to believe. The message of *The Outsider* is, hopefully, that a new, more honest era is beginning for the Irish-American image on American screens.

Notes

I. Native Irish Film Production

1. Ringsend, now a southeastern suburb of Dublin, was a riverside village, where the River Dodder flows into the Liffey, between the Dublin city center and the sea.
2. In a letter to the author, September 10, 1968.
3. Reprinted as an advertisement for *Knocknagow* in the February 1918 issue of *Irish Limelight*.
4. *Willy Reilly and His Colleen Bawn* and *Knocknagow* are both preserved in the National Film Archive, London.
5. Extract from John McDonagh's reminiscences, published in *Cinema Ireland 1895–1976*, Dublin Arts Festival, 1976, p. 11.
6. *The Bioscope*, July 12, 1917.
7. N. Ormsby-Smith in a letter to the Selig Polyscope Company, London, January 15, 1918, in the Selig Collection at the Academy of Motion Picture Arts and Sciences.
8. Kevin Rockett, "Film Censorship & the State," *Film Directions*, Vol. III, No. 9, 1980, p. 12.
9. Hubert H. Tiltman, "Ireland—A Film El Dorado!" *Picture Plays*, January 10, 1920, p. 23.
10. In a letter to the author, September 10, 1968.
11. *Irish Destiny* is preserved in the National Film Collection at the Library of Congress.
12. Quoted in Gloria Emerson, "Film Takes the Irish Down 'Rocky Road'," *Los Angeles Herald-Examiner*, July 21, 1968, p. G-4. Lennon is also the subject of two unsigned pieces, "Was the Irish Rebellion Really Fought in Vain?" and "How Lennon Got around Censors and Taboos," in *Life*, July 22, 1968, pp. 5–6. *Rocky Road to Dublin* was produced by Victor Herbert and released in the United States in 1968, following its presentation at the Cannes Film Festival.
13. Quoted in Julie Richard, "Trouble in Northern Ireland: What's Fact, What's Fiction?" *Los Angeles Times*, Calendar, December 2, 1984, p. 23.
14. *Ibid*.

II. The American Film Producer in Ireland

1. *Daydreams*. London: Hurst and Blackett, 1923.
2. George Blaisdell, "Irish History on the Screen," *The Moving Picture World*, August 29, 1914, p. 1245.
3. *Variety*, October 10, 1914.
4. Robert C. McElravy in *The Moving Picture World*, October 3, 1914, p. 67.

5. *Photoplay*, April 1930, p. 53.
6. *The Hills of Ireland* campaign book, p. 2.
7. Norris Davidson, "Ireland Shapes New Film Policy," *World Film News*, October 1936, p. 9.

III. Irish Literature and the Cinema

1. Bryan Forbes, *Dame Edith Evans: Ned's Girl*, Little, Brown, 1977, p. 195.
2. Quoted in Maurice Desmond, "Mr. Shaw and the Movies," *Shadowland*, March–April 1920, p. 47.
3. Quoted in Archibald Henderson, *Table-Talk of G.B.S.*, Chapman & Hall, 1925, p. 65.
4. Quoted in Donald P. Costello, *The Serpent's Eye*, University of Notre Dame Press, 1965, p. 42.
5. Reproduced in *Sight and Sound*, August–September 1951, p. 10.
6. Micheál Mac Liammóir, *Theatre in Ireland*, Cultural Relations Committee of Ireland, 1950, p. 44.

IV. The Irishman in Hollywood

1. Johnstone Craig, "The Dominant Race," *Photoplay*, October 1918, p. 48.
2. Scott Eyman, "Just an Irish Show Off," *Films and Filming*, April 1982, p. 13.
3. *Ibid*, p. 15.
4. Donn Byrne, *Hangman's House*, The Century Co., 1926, pp. viii–ix.
5. Lindsay Anderson, "The Quiet Man," *Sequence*, No. 14, New Year, 1952, p. 24.
6. In a letter to the author dated June 23, 1975, Vernon Harbin of RKO Radio Pictures explained that RKO's rights in the film expired on or about May 22, 1945, and reverted to Sean O'Casey. He also confirmed that retakes and added scenes were photographed by George Nicholls, Jr., but that only Ford received credit on the screen and in advertising.
7. Herbert Wilcox, *Twenty-Five Thousand Sunsets*, A.S. Barnes, 1969, p. 30.
8. Julian Johnson, "Clan Moore," *Photoplay*, December 1918, p. 27.
9. *Ibid*, p. 28.
10. Des Hickey and Gus Smith, *A Paler Shade of Green*, Leslie Frewin, p. 243.
11. Micheál Mac Liammóir, *All for Hecuba*, Branden Press, 1967, p. 163.
12. In a letter to the author, dated August 8, 1968.
13. Micheál Ó hAodha, *Theatre in Ireland*, Rowman and Littlefield, 1974, p. 50.
14. *The Sunday Times* [London]. February 17, 1937.

V. The Irish Image on American Screens

1. For more information on Sir Roger Casement, a fascinating character, see *Roger Casement* by Brian Inglis, published by Harcourt Brace Jovanovich, 1974. Inglis points out that Casement was executed more because he was a homosexual than an Irish patriot.
2. *Exhibitor's Trade Review*, January 27, 1917, p. 575.
3. Reprinted in *The Film Mercury*, July 16, 1927, p. 12.
4. Bob Callahan, "The Making of 'The Outsider'," *Callahan's Irish Quarterly*, Winter 1981, p. 60.

Bibliography

Anderson, Lindsay, "The Quiet Man," *Sequence*, No. 14, New Year, 1952, pp. 23-27.
"'Angel' May Signal Rebirth for Irish; Govt. Boosts Ante," *Variety*, June 2, 1982, pp. 5 and 32.
Bell, Sam Hanna. *The Theatre in Ulster*. Totowa, New Jersey: Rowman and Littlefield, 1972.
Blaisdell, George, "Irish History on the Screen," *The Moving Picture World*, August 29, 1914, p. 1245.
Blume, Mary, "'MacHuston' Films Scotland in Erin," *Los Angeles Times*, Part IV, August 18, 1967, p. 22.
Bogdanovich, Peter. *John Ford*. Berkeley: University of California Press, 1968.
Boone, J. Allen, "Finding a Personality," *Motion Picture Classic*, January 1916, pp. 43-46.
"A Bunch of Talent," *The Cinema*, July 2, 1914, p. 9.
Byrne, Donn. *Hangman's House*. New York: The Century Co., 1926.
"Censors in Eire Concentrate on Keeping Neutral," *Motion Picture Herald*, December 11, 1943, p. 32.
Cinema Ireland 1895-1976. Dublin: Dublin Arts Festival, 1976.
Clark, Dennis, "The Irish in the Movies: A Tradition of Permanent Blur," in *Ethnic Images in American Film and Television*, ed. by Randall M. Miller. Philadelphia: Public Papers in the Humanities, No. 1/The Balch Institute, 1978.
Comiskey, Ray, "New Images on Screen," *Ireland of the Welcomes*, September-October 1985, pp. 36-39.
Costello, Donald P. *The Serpent's Eye*. Notre Dame: University of Notre Dame Press, 1965.
Coxhead, Elizabeth. *Daughters of Erin*. London: Secker and Warburg, 1965.
Craig, Johnstone, "The Dominant Race," *Photoplay*, October 1918, pp. 48 and 112.
Davidson, Norris, "Ireland Shapes New Film Policy," *World Film News*, October 1936, p. 9.
Desmond, Maurice, "Mr. Shaw and the Movies," *Shadowland*, Vol. II, Nos. 7-8, March-April 1920, p. 47.
Dooley, Roger B., "The Irish on the Screen: I," *Films in Review*, Vol. VIII, No. 5, May 1957, pp. 211-217.
_____, "The Irish on the Screen: II," *Films in Review*, Vol. VIII, No. 6, June-July 1957, pp. 259-270.
Downing, Taylor, "The Film Company of Ireland," *Sight and Sound*, Vol. XLIX, No. 1, Winter 1979/80, pp. 42-45.
Eyman, Scott, "Just an Irish Show-Off," *Films and Filming*, April 1982, pp. 11-15.
Fox, Julian, "Maureen O'Hara: The Fighting Lady," *Films and Filming*, December 1972, pp. 32-40.

Gaddis, Pearl, "Blazing a Trail in the Movies," *Photoplay*, September 1914, pp. 104–107.
Galligan, Richard, "Irish Like Their Flicks Clean, Simple—and Old," *Los Angeles Times*, Part X, September 22, 1974, pp. 1 and 10.
"Gauntier Feature Players," *The Moving Picture World*, December 21, 1912, p. 1169.
Geltzer, George, "Herbert Brenon," *Films in Review*, Vol. VI, No. 3, March 1955, pp. 116–125.
Gifford, Denis. *The British Film Catalogue, 1895–1970*. New York: McGraw-Hill, 1973.
———. *The Illustrated Who's Who in British Films*. London: B.T. Batsford, 1978.
Gorham, Maurice. *Forty Years of Irish Broadcasting*. Dublin: The Talbot Press, 1967.
Green, Alice, "Fighting Irishman," *Film Weekly*, January 9, 1937, p. 26.
Henderson, Archibald. *Table-Talk of G.B.S.* London: Chapman & Hall, 1925.
Hickey, Des and Gus Smith. *A Paler Shade of Green*. London: Leslie Frewin, 1972.
Hunt, Hugh. *The Abbey: Ireland's National Theatre, 1904–1978*. New York: Columbia University Press, 1979.
Hutchins, Patricia, "James Joyce and the Cinema," *Sight and Sound*, Vol. XXI, No. 1, August–September 1951, pp. 9 and 11–12.
"Ireland's Ardmore Studios," *American Cinematographer*, August 1969, pp. 776–777 and 799.
Johnson, Julian, "Clan Moore," *Photoplay*, December 1918, pp. 27–29 and 107.
Johnston, Denis, "The Last Refuge of Nationality," *Film Art*, Autumn 1935, pp. 63–64.
Joseph, Robert, "Films Come to the Emerald Isle," *Los Angeles Times*, Calendar, March 17, 1968, pp. 26 and 64.
Lewis, Frank, "Hollywood in Beaufort," *Ireland of the Welcomes*, July–August 1978, pp. 14–17.
McGowan, J.P., "O'Kalems Return to Ireland," *The Moving Picture World*, August 10, 1912, p. 537.
MacKillop, James, "Ireland and the Movies: From the Volta Cinema to RTÉ," *Éire-Ireland*, Vol. XIX, No. 2, 1984, pp. 7–22.
Mac Liammóir, Micheál. *Theatre in Ireland*. Dublin: Cultural Relations Committee of Ireland, 1950.
———. *Put Money in Thy Purse*. London: Methuen, 1952.
———. *Each Actor on His Ass*. London: Routledge and Kegan Paul, 1961.
———. *All for Hecuba*. Boston: Branden Press, 1967.
———. *An Oscar of No Importance*. London: Heinemann, 1968.
MacLochlain, Alf, "Ireland a Nation," *Scannán*, February 1966, pp. 7–9.
Mapes, Agnes, "A Kalem Girl in Ireland," *The Moving Picture World*, July 15, 1911, p. 31.
"Milo O'Shea," *Current Biography*, June 1982, pp. 33–36.
Molony, Mick, "Stereotypes in the Media: The Irish-American Case," in *Ethnic Images in American Film and Television*, ed. by Randall M. Miller. Philadelphia: Public Papers in the Humanities, No. 1/The Balch Institute, 1978.
Moriarty, Kevin, "Fixed Assets," *Film Directions*, Vol. II, No. 8, 1979, pp. 4–5.
Munden, Kenneth, ed. *American Film Institute Catalog: Feature Films 1921–1930*. New York: R.R. Bowker, 1971.
Nicholson, Constance H., "Films About Irish Authors," *Film News*, February/March 1969, pp. 6–9 and 31.
O Conluain, Proinsias, "Ireland's First Films," *Sight and Sound*, Vol. XXIII, No. 2, October/December 1953, pp. 96–98.
———. *Scéal na Scannán*. Dublin: Oifig an tSoláthair, 1953.

Ó hAodha, Micheál. *Theatre in Ireland*. Totowa, New Jersey: Rowman and Littlefield, 1974.
O Laoghaire, Liam. *Invitation to the Film*. Tralee, Ireland: The Kerryman Ltd., 1945.
O'Leary, Liam, "The Cinema in Ireland," *The Word*, March 1976, pp. 3-7.
_____. *Rex Ingram: Master of the Silent Cinema*. New York: Barnes & Noble, 1980.
_____. *A Seat Among the Stars: The Cinema and Ireland*. Belfast: Ulster Television, 1984.
Reynolds, Horace, "Hollywood Unfurls the Plough and the Stars," *Stage*, February 1937, unpaged.
Richard, Julie, "Trouble in Northern Ireland: What's Fact, What's Fiction?" *Los Angeles Times*, Calendar, December 2, 1984, pp. 23-24.
Roberts, Glyn, "Ireland Still Waits," *Film Weekly*, July 23, 1938, pp. 10-11.
Rockett, Kevin, "Caoineadh Airt Ui Laoire," *Film Directions*, Vol. I, No. 1, 1977, pp. 18-19.
_____, "Constructing a Film Culture: Ireland," *Screen Education*, Summer 1978, pp. 23-33.
_____, "Irish Cinema: Notes on Some Nationalist Fictions," *Screen*, Vol. XX, Nos. 3-4, Winter 1979-80, pp. 115-123.
_____, "Film Censorship & the State," *Film Directions*, Vol. III, No. 9, 1980, pp. 11-15.
_____, "Stars Get in Your Eyes," *Framework*, No. 25, 1984, pp. 28-41.
Sharpe, Howard, "Beginning Bright," *Photoplay*, June 1939, pp. 22-24 and 77.
_____, "Bright Victory," *Photoplay*, July 1939, pp. 66-67 and 87-88.
Sheehy, T.J.M., "Towards That Irish Film Industry," *The Irish Digest*, December 1948, pp. 7-9.
_____, "Huston Urges Ireland Develop Film Industry," *Motion Picture Herald*, October 11, 1967, pp. 12 and 14.
Slide, Anthony, "The Colleen Bawn," *Vision*, Spring 1967, pp. 22-23.
_____, "The O'Kalems," *Cinema Studies*, Vol. II, No. 5, September 1967, pp. 77-79.
_____, "The Silent Cinema and Ireland," *Vision*, Autumn 1967, p. 20.
_____, "Sara Allgood," *Film Fan Monthly*, June 1970, pp. 15-17.
Tiltman, Hubert H., "Ireland—A Film El Dorado!," *Picture Plays*, January 10, 1920, p. 23.
Vaines, Colin, "Too Little, Too Late," *Screen International*, April 14, 1979, p. 16.
_____, "'Cal' Subject Matter Proves David Puttnam with Many Attractions," *Screen International*, May 19, 1984, p. 15.
Wilcox, Herbert. *Twenty-Five Thousand Sunsets*. New York: A.S. Barnes, 1969.

Index

A

Abbey Theatre 22, 29, 30, 32, 90, 91, 94, 95, 96, 97, 98
Abbey Theatre School 89
Abie's Irish Rose 101
Act without Words II 65
Adorée, Renée 65
Adrian, Max 88
"The Adventures of Peaceful Rafferty" series 103
The Adventures of Robinson Crusoe 90
Aimsir Padraig 9
Ainley, Henry 53
Albright, Ivan and Malvin 55
Alexander, Frances 14
All-Celtic Company 102–103
Allen, Ira 9
Allgood, Sara 22, 94–95
Alpha Trading Company 2
Altman, Robert 49
Anderson, Michael 30
Andrews, Eamonn 33
Andrews, Julie 64
Androcles and the Lion 60, 61
Angel 35, 36
Angels with Dirty Faces 76
Anna Karenina 91
Annabella 47
Anne Devlin 34–35
Anne of Green Gables 84
Annie Laurie 87
Ardmore Studios 28–32, 34
Arise My Love 92
Arms and the Man 58, 62
Armstrong, Robert 76
Armstrong, Will 101
Around the Corner 108
Around the World in Eighty Days 92

Arrah-na-Pogue 42
Arvidson, Linda 87
Asquith, Anthony 56, 57, 60, 62
Astaire, Fred 113
Atkins, Christopher 65
Ault, Marie 17
Axt, William 60
Aylmer, Felix 62

B

Bacon, Lloyd 109
Baddeley, Angela 58
Baggott, King 102
Balderston, John 109
Ball, Ernest R. 74
The Ballroom of Romance 36
Banba Company 11
Bank Holiday 20
Bara, Theda 85, 104
Barker, Florence 53
Baroud 85
The Barretts of Wimpole Street 89, 98
Barriscale, Bessie 103
Barry Lyndon 49
Barrymore, Ethel 73
Barrymore, John 73
Barrymore, Lionel 73
Beat the Devil 92
Beau Geste 85, 93
Beaufort, Killarney 40–43
Beckett, Samuel 65–65
Beckett 91
Bed and Board 107
Beering, Kathleen E. 87
Behan, Brendan 32, 33, 64
Behrman, S.N. 110
Belfast 34, 37

Belfast Arts Theatre 93
Belfast Repertory Company 93
Belfast Repertory Theatre 21
Bellamy, Eileen 16
Bellamy, Madge 107
Belles of Killarney 4
Belmont Theatre, New York 26
Beloved Enemy 109
Benchley, Robert 54, 108
Benedict, Phil 7
Ben-Hur 93
Bennett, Belle 73
Berger, Helmut 55
Berger, Ludwig 59
Bernstein, Morey 111
Bessada, Milad 37
Beverly of Graustark 87
The Bible 51, 93
The Big Birthday 32
The Big Gamble 111
Das Bildnis des Dorian Gray 5
Binney, Constance 107
Birmingham, George A. 17
Biro, Lajos 55
Black, Cathal 38
Black Oxen 66
Blackmail 94
Blackton, J. Stuart 104, 105
Blair, Betsy 32
Blakely, Colin 93
Blarney 26, 65
The Blarney Stone 43
Blood from the Mummy's Tomb 63
The Blue Lagoon 65
Bogarde, Dirk 62
Bohemian Theatre, Dublin 9, 12
Bold Emmett, Ireland's Martyr 43
Bombardier 76
Bond, Derek 63
Boone, Pat 112
Boorman, John 31, 35, 49
Borzage, Frank 46
Bosworth, Hobart 65, 78
Boucicault, Dion 17, 42, 74, 107
Bouwmeester, Lily 59
Box, Muriel 32
The Boy and the Bridge 92
Boyd, Dorothy 17
Boyd, Stephen 111
Boyer, Charles 54
Brabin, Charles 104
Brady, Cyrus Townsend 104, 105

Branwell Film Productions 109
Brendan Behan's Dublin 72
Brennan, Jimmy 38
Brennan o' the Moor 103
Brenon, Herbert 85
Brent, George 89
Brett, Jeremy 63
Brian, Mary 85
The Bride Came C.O.D. 87
Bride of Frankenstein 93, 98
The Bride's Play 65, 107
Bridges Burned 104
British Film Institute 34
Brogan, Harry 29, 32
Bronson, Betty 85
Brosnan, Pierce 92
Broth of a Boy 32
Browning, Tod 63, 104
Brunton, Robert 104
Bryant, Charles 55
Buel, Kenean 54
Bullet Scars 87
Bunny, John 43
Burke, Brenda 12
Burke, Johnny 110
Burke, Marie 49
Burke 14
Burnett, W.R. 110
Bushman, Francis X. 73
Bute, Mary Ellen 68
Butler, W. 15
By Accident 20
Byrne, Eddie 89

C

Caesar and Cleopatra 60, 61
Cagney, James 30, 75, 76, 109
Cal 36–37
Caldwell, Anne 107
The Callahans and the Murphys 107–108
Camelot 91
Cameron, Sir Charles 5
The Canterville Ghost 55
Capitol Cinema, Dublin 19, 24
Captain Blood 75
Captain Lightfoot 110–111
Cardiff, Jack 69, 84

The Cardinal 113
Cardinall, Mrs. Alice 9
Carey, Macdonald 32
Carey, Patrick 33, 66
Carleton, William 14
Carnduff, Tom 21
Caron, Leslie 62
Carroll, Madeleine 54
Carroll, Nancy 101
Carstairs, John Paddy 32
Carter, Angela 38
Casement, Sir Roger 104
Casey, Patrick 5
Casey's Millions 10
Cashel Byron's Profession 57
Casino Royale 51
Castles for Two 104
The Cat and the Canary 86, 87
Catholics: A Fable 63–64
A Cattle Drive in County Galway 4
Cavalcade 98
CBS "Playhouse 90" 64
Cellier, Antoinette 23
Celtic Film Company 18
Celtic Photoplays, Inc. 18
Censorship 15–16
The Ceremony 113
Chaffey, Don 32
Channel 4 35
Chapman, Edward 95
Charity 87
Cheaper by the Dozen 95
Chekhov, Michael 101
Children at Work 33
Children's Committee 10 37
The Children's Folk Dancing Fete 11
Christian Brothers 38
Christie, Julie 83
City of James Joyce 72
Clancey, Nora 13
Clancy, Carl Stearns 46
Clancy's Kosher Wedding 101
Clark, Jack 41, 103
Clark, Marguerite 103
Clark, May 8
Clark, Petula 113
Clifford, Tom 108
Clifford, Tommy 47
Cluny Brown 95
Clyde, Andy 107
Cohan, George M. 73
Cohen, Norman 72

The Cohens and the Kellys 101–102
"The Cohens and the Kellys" series 102
Colebourne, Maurice 58
Coleman, Vincent 106
Colleen 107
The Colleen Bawn (1912) 42
The Colleen Bawn (1924) 17
Collier, Constance 56
Collinge, Lenny 67–68
Collins, Michael 109
Collyer, June 65, 78
Colman, Ronald 55
Come Back to Erin 43
The Company of Wolves 38
Compton, Fay 34, 55
Conklin, Chester 107
Connolly, Walter 74
Connor, Mary 18
Conquest of Light 33
Cook, Fielder 29, 30
Coop, Denys 50
Cooper, Gladys 63
Cooper, Tom 24–26
Coppola, Francis Ford 113
Cork and Vicinity 43
A Corner in Colleens 103
Costello, Dolores 107
The Court Film 9
Court Laundry 9
Courtenay, Tom 54
Coutard, Raoul 34
Coventry, Tom 16
Cowan, Jerome 109
Cox, Charles 43
Cox, George 43
Crane, Frank Hart 53
Crawford, Joan 110
Creation Film Company 106
Crime by Night 87
Crisp, Donald 109
Crosby, Bing 75, 101, 110
Crossfire 37
Crowden, Graham 38
Crowe, Eileen 29, 30, 82, 83, 96–97, 110
Cruiskeen Lawn 10–11
The Cry of Erin 103
Cukor, George 95
Cummings, Robert 54
Cunard, Grace 103
Curley, Mayor James M. 105
Curzon Theatre, Dublin 70

Cusack, Cyril 13, 19, 30, 34, 38, 65, 66, 83, 89

D

Dallamano, Massimo 55
Dalrymple, Andrew Argus 37
Dalton, Audrey 32
Dalton, Dorothy 73
Dalton, Emmet 28–30, 32
Dalton, Geoffrey 19
Damhsa Arann 20
Dance Girl Dance 89
Dangerous Hours 65
Danny Boy 35–36
Darby O'Gill and the Little People 26, 91
Dark Moon Hollow 34
Darling Lili 49
Dassin, Jules 55
A Daughter of Erin 99–100
A Daughter of the Gods 85
David Copperfield 89
Davidson, Norris 20, 52
Davies, Marion 107
Davis, Bill C. 92
Davis, Charles 33
Davis, Eileen 24
Davison, Philip 37
Dawley, J. Searle 103
The Dawn 24–26
Dawn over Ireland 25
de Havilland, Olivia 109
Delaney, Maureen 18
De Marney, Derrick 63
de Messter, John 59
Dempsey, Michael 19
Denison, Michael 56
Denny from Ireland 104
Denvers, John 18
de Putti, Lya 79
De Sarno, Marcel 65
de Sica, Vittorio 62
Desmond, William 88
Devane, William 113
de Vere Stacpoole, Henry 65
The Devil's Agent 32
Dexter, Elliott 104
Dirrane, Maggie 49

Disney, Walt 91
The Doctor's Dilemma 62
Domino Company 102
Donath, Ludwig 64
Donlevy, Brian 93
Donn-Byrne, Brian Oswald 65, 78, 107, 108
Donovan, Fred 12
The Doorway of Destruction 76
Doro, Marie 104
Douglas, Ethel 16
Douglas, Kirk 62
Dowlan, William 103
Dracula, or the Un-Dead 63
Dreams of Toyland 2
Dressler, Marie 107
Drogheda, Republic of Ireland 36
Dru, Joanne 101
Drumcollogher Fire 46
Drums along the Mohawk 98
Dublin and Nearby 45
Dublin Film Company 27
The Duchess 103
Duffy, Gerard 26
Duffy, John 26
Dugan, Harry 49
Du Maurier, Daphne 23
Dunn, James 75
Dunne, Rev. Joseph 33
Duvivier, Julian 54

E

Earle, William P.S. 104
The Early Bird 21
Edwards, Blake 49
Edwards, Hilton 28, 32
Eiline of Erin 102
Eire Films, Ltd. 28
Eisenstein, Sergei 68
The Eleventh Hour 14
Ellenshaw, Peter 91
Elliman, Louis 28, 33
Eltinge, Julian 73
Elvey, Maurice 17, 54
Empire Variety Theatre, Belfast 1
Engel, Erich 59
Englund, Ken 61
Enigma Company 36

Eppel, Dr. I.J. 18
Erskine, Chester 61
Evans, Clifford 23
Evans, Edith 56, 57
Evans, Maurice 61
Excalibur 49
The Exploits of Elaine 86
Exposure 37

F

Fahay, Rev. William J. 108
Faithful Departed 72
The Fall of the Roman Empire 93
Fallon, Gabriel 26
Farnham, Allen 41
Farnum, Dustin 73, 103
Farnum, William 73
Farrar, Geraldine 73
Farrell, Alderman J.J. 68
Fascination 87
Father O'Flynn 16
Fenton, Leslie 78
Field, Betty 54
Fields, Gracie 22–23
Fighting Father Dunne 76
The Fighting Prince of Donegal 112
The Fighting 69th 76
Film 64
Film Company of Ireland 11–14
Financing the Irish Republic 45
Finch, Peter 66
Finglas Fair Day 11
Finian's Rainbow 113
Finnegans Wake 68
The First National Pilgrimage to Lourdes 5
Fischer, O.W. 62
Fisher, Lawrence 106
Fitzgerald, Barry 18, 19, 32, 75, 82, 94, 95, 97–98, 110
Fitzgerald, J.A. 103
Fitzgibbon, Henry 12
Fitzpatrick, James 46
Flaherty, Robert 48–49
Flanagan, John 23
Flanagan, Fionnula 71–72
Flavin, Rev. J.F. 17
Fleischer, Max 53

Fleming, Victor 101
Flemyng, Gordon 62
Flesh and Fantasy 54
Fonda, Henry 47
Food of Love 14
Foolish Matrons 65
For Ireland's Sake 43
For the Freedom of Ireland 106–107
For the Wearing of the Green 102
Ford, Cecil 26
Ford, Francis 76, 103
Ford, John 65, 76–84, 89, 103, 108
Forster, Ralph 16
Fort Apache 75
Forty-Five Minutes in Ireland 45
Foss, Kenelm 16
Foster, Barry 37
Foster, Preston 82
The Four Horsemen of the Apocalypse 85
Four Provinces Films, Ltd. 83
Fox, Reginald 16
The Fox of Glenarvon 27
Foy, Pat 103
Frank, Charles 63
Franken, Rose 109
Frau Warrens Geharbe 62
Friel, Brian 63
The Front Page 75
Der Fuchs von Glenarvon 27
Furbay, John H. 28

G

Gable, Clark 110
Gaelic Amusement Company 45
Gael-Linn 33
Gaffney, Liam 21
Gail, Jane 54
The Garden of Allah 15
Gardiner, Reginald 61
Garnett, Tay 34
Garrick, John 17, 47
Garson, Greer 93
Gate Theatre 19, 28, 90
Gauntier, Gene 40, 41, 43, 103
Gaynor, Janet 78, 108
General John Regan 17
Gielgud, John 56, 61, 70

Gill, Basil 54
Gillstrom, Arvid E. 101
Gilmore, Lowell 55
A Girl of Glenbeigh 12
Girl with Green Eyes 96
Gish, Dorothy 73
Gish, Lillian 73
Glazer, Benjamin 92
Glazier, Sidney 64
Gleeson, James 24, 75, 76
Glennon, Bert 108
Goddard, Paulette 56
Going My Way 98
Gold, Jack 64
Goldsmith, Oliver 53-54
Goldwyn, Sam 63, 109
Goodbye, Mr. Chips 93
Gordon, Mary 109
Gordon, Vera 102
Grahame, Margot 81
Grand Cinema, Dublin 14
Grand Opera House, Belfast 1
Grant, Valentine 43
Graves, Ralph 65
Great Catherine 62
Great Expectations 93
The Great Gatsby 85
The Great McGinty 93
The Great Victor Herbert 74
Great Western Railway Company 2, 4
Greco, Juliette 111
Green, Gilbert 9
Greene, Graham 61, 62
Greenwood, Joan 56, 57
Gregory, Lady 83
Grieve, Harold 55
Griffith, Corinne 66
Griffith, D.W. 87
Grimes, Stephen 50
Groh, David 113
Guests of the Nation 19
Guinan, Texas 73
Guitry, Sacha 68
Gulliver No Uchu Ryoko 53
Gulliver's Travels 53
Gulliver's Travels Beyond the Moon 53
Guthrie, Tyrone 81
Gwenn, Edmund 58

H

Haddick, Col. Victor 20, 26
Haines, Fred 68
Hale, Creighton 86-88
Hamilton, Guy 62
Hamilton, Shorty 104
Hammer Films 63
Hampton, Hope 55
Hangman's House 65, 75, 78-79, 108
Hanson, Lars 79
The Happiest Millionaire 113
The Happy Prince 54
Harburg, E.Y. 81, 113
Hare, Sir John 53
A Harp in Hock 102
Harris, Julie 32
Harris, Richard 34, 53, 91, 109, 113
Harris, Robert 58
Harrison, Eric 16
Harrison, Rex 60, 63
Harron, Robert 73, 103
Harryhausen, Ray 53
Harvey, Lawrence 113
Haskell, Peter 68
Hasse, O.E. 62
Hatfield, Hurd 55
Hawkins, Jack 62
Hayden, Sterling 113
Haye, Helen 48
Hayes, Mairin 19
Haymes, Dick 74
Hayward, Richard 20, 21
Hecht-Hill-Lancaster 62
Heerman, Victor 39, 40
Helden 62
Henry V 28
Henson, Gerald 94
Hepburn, Audrey 63
Hepburn, Katharine 62
Herbert, Victor 74
Here Is Ireland 27
The Heritage of Ireland 33
Hersholt, Jean 101
Heywood, Anne 34
Hibernia Film Studios 24
Hickey, Kieran 33, 37, 72
Hill, Colin 34
Hill, George 107
Hiller, Wendy 60

The Hills of Ireland 49
His Captive Woman 65
His Own People 104
Hitchcock, Alfred 64, 94
Hobson, Valerie 93
Hoffman, Aaron 101
Hogan, Bosco 70
Hollister, Alice 41
Hollister, George 40
Holloway, Joseph 45
Holloway, Stanley 17, 63
Hollywood Boulevard 87
Holmes, Burton 45
Home Is the Hero 29–30, 96
Honegger, Arthur 60
Hopson, Violet 53
Horgan, James 1
Horgan, Philip 1
Horgan, Thomas 1–2
Horgan's Picture Palace 2
Horseman, Pass By 66
The Housemaster 85
Houston, Donald 65
How Green Was My Valley 75, 82, 89, 95, 98
How He Lied to Her Husband 58
How the Myth Was Made 48
Howard, Leslie 60
Howard, Trevor 50, 64
Huckleberry Finn 84
Hudson, Rock 110
The Hunchback of Notre Dame 89
Hungry Hill 23, 90, 93, 96, 97
Hunter, Ross 110
Hurley, John 18
Hurst, Brian Desmond 22–24, 83
Hurst's Picture Palace, Youghal 2
Huston, John 51–52, 70, 92
Hyde-White, Wilfrid 63

I

IRA 19, 23, 24, 34, 36, 79, 89, 113–114
An Ideal Husband 55–56
The Idol Dancer 87
Images 49
The Importance of Being Earnest 56–57

In Old Chicago 74
In Old Ireland 45
In the Days of St. Patrick 8–19
The Informer 75, 79–81, 98
Ingram, Rex 85
The Inheritance 63
The Invisible Man 98
Ireland a Nation 44–45
Ireland and Israel 100
Ireland in Revolt 46
Ireland, the Melody Isle 46
Ireland the Oppressed 42
"Ireland Today" 4
Ireland Today 10, 28
Ireland's Border Line 26
Irish and Proud of It 21
The Irish Blacksmith 99
The Irish Cloth Industry 5
Irish Destiny 18–19
Irish Events 9
Irish Eyes 103
Irish Eyes Are Smiling 74
Irish Film Board 32, 35
Irish for Luck 22
An Irish Girl's Love 102
Irish Hearts 22
The Irish Honeymoon 41
The Irish in America 43
The Irish in Us 109
Irish Life 5
Irish Luck 39–40
"Irish Mafia" 76, 109
Irish National Film Corporation 26
Irish Photoplays, Ltd. 10
The Irish Rebel 43
Irish Republican Army, see IRA
Irish Whiskey Rebellion 113
Irish Wives and English Husbands 4
Irwin, Walter W. 105
It Happened in Flatbush 95
It's Love Again 95
It's Not the Size That Counts 92

J

Jackson, Mary 34
Jamaica Inn 89
James Joyce's Women 72
Jefferson, William Winter 54

Jefford, Barbara 69
Jeffs, Fred 10
Jenkins, Allen 76
The Jewel of the Seven Stars 63
Johanna Enlists 84
Johns, Glynis 30, 56
Johnson, Page 68
Johnston, Denis 19
Jolas, Maria 68
Jolly, Professor 1
Jones, Christopher 50
Jordan, Neil 35, 36, 38
Joyce, Alice 47, 88, 104
Joyce, James 66–72
Joyce, Paul 65
Judge, Peter 96–97
Jugo, Jenny 59
Juno and the Paycock 93, 94–95, 97
Just Peggy 94

Kershner, Irwin 63
Kickham, Charles 13
Kidder, Margot 37
Killanin, Lord Michael 83
Kimmich, Max W. 27
Kind Hearts and Coronets 93
King, Joe 103
The King of Kings 93
The King of the Threshold 94
A Kiss for Cinderella 85
Kleiser, Randal 65
Klugston, Robert 106
Knocknagow 13–14
Knowles, Patric 22
Knute Rockne — All American 76
Korda, Alexander 55, 56
Kosher Kitty Kelly 102
The Kreutzer Sonata 85
Kubrick, Stanley 49

K

Kalem Company 40–43, 54
Kane, Robert T. 47
Kathleen Mavourneen 95, 99, 104, 107
Kaufman, Boris 64
Kavanagh, H.T. 91
Kay, William 14
Keating, Alice 9, 13
Keaton, Buster 64
Keefe, Zena 87
Keith, Brian 113
Kellermann, Annette 85
Kellino, W.P. 17
Kelly, Martin J. 68
Kelly, Patsy 75
Kelly, Walter C. 107
Kelly's Hotel, Rosslare 3
Kelvin Film Company 10
Kennedy, Arthur 29, 30
Kennedy's Ireland 33
Kenny, Sean 109
Kent, Charles 104
Kent, Larry 65, 78, 107
Keogh, Des 51
Kerr, Deborah 60
Kerrigan, J.M. 47, 82, 94, 97, 101
Kerrigan, J. Warren 73, 104
The Kerry Gow 42

L

Lacy, Kate 3
The Lad from Old Ireland 41
Lady Windermere's Fan 55, 56
Lamont, Molly 22
Lancaster, Burt 62
Land of Her Fathers 18
Lane, Burton 81, 113
Langley, Noel 111
Lansbury, Angela 38, 55
The Last Dance 108
The Last Hurrah 75
Laughton, Charles 55, 89
Launder, Frank 65
Lawrence, William Mervyn 72
Lawrence of Arabia 91
Lawson, Wilfred 60
Leah, Frank 9
Lean, David 49, 50
Leave It to the Irish 75
Leaves from Nature's Books, No. 3 5
Le Clair, Professor 1
Lee, Anna 79
Lee, Christopher 32
Le Fanu, Sheridan 63
Leigh, Vivien 61
Leinen aus Irland 27–28
Leinster, Colin 113

Lennon, Councillor P. 15
Lennon, Peter 33–34
Lennox, Vera 58
Leonard, Hugh 32, 91
Lerner, Alan Jay 63
Leslie, Gladys 104
A Letter from Ulster 23
Lewin, Albert 55
Lewis, Cecil 58
Lewis, J. Gordon 8, 9
Lewis, Sheldon 87
Lies My Father Told Me 32
The Life of St. Patrick 5–8
Lily of Killarney 17
Limerick County Council 83
Linen from Ireland 27–28
Linihan, Rosaleen 70
The Lion in Winter 91
Lipman, Joe 94
The List of Adrian Messenger 51
The Little Irish Girl 107
Little Lady Eileen 103
"Little Rex" 16
The Little Runaway 104
Lloyd, Frederick 58
Lloyd, James 1
Lockwood, Margaret 22, 23
Loder, John 23
Lodge, John 23
Loewe, Frederick 63
Lohr, Marie 60
Lom, Herbert 55
London to Killarney 3–4
The Lonely Girl 66
Long Day's Journey into Night 113
The Long Good Friday 92
The Long Gray Line 74
The Long, Hot Summer 91
The Long Voyage Home 82
Lord Arthur Saville's Crime and Other Stories 54
The Lord Loves the Irish 104
Loren, Sophia 62
Love, Bessie 62
Lover, Samuel 102
The Loves of Cass McGuire 63
Lowe, Victoria 87
Lowrey, Dan 1
Loy, Myrna 110
Lubitsch, Ernst 55
The Luck of Ginger Coffey 63
Luck of the Irish 21

The Luck of the Irish 74
Lugosi, Bela 63
Lumley, Mabelle 43
Luraschi, Tony 113
Lynch, Christopher 49
Lynch, John 36
Lyric Players Theatre, Belfast 93

M

MacArthur 91
McAvoy, May 55
Macbeth 90
McBride, Sean 66
McCann, Donald 112
McCarey, Leo 108
McCarthy, Dermot 9
McCarthy, Johnny 24
McClintock, Libby 63
McClory, Kevin 92, 109
McCormack, John 40, 46–48, 49
McCormick, F.J. 11, 23, 34, 82, 94, 96–97
MacDermott, Marc 104
McDonagh, John 10
MacDonald, J. Farrell 47, 75, 78, 79, 101, 102, 109
MacDonnell, Barrett 10
McDonogh, Miss B.J. 5
McDonough, John 14
McEnery, Peter 112
McEvoy, C.A. 11
McFadden's Flats 107
McGarvey, Cathal 19
MacGinnis, Niall 21, 23, 24, 30, 32
McGoohan, Patrick 32
McGowan, Brian 12, 13, 14, 19
McGowan, J.P. 41
MacGowran, Jack 72, 83, 91
McHugh, Frank 76, 109
McHugh, Michael J. 83
Macken, Walter 29, 30, 32
Mackendrick, Alexander 62
McKenna, Siobhán 23, 24, 66, 93
McKenna, T.P. 69, 70, 113
The McKenzie Break 113
McKern, Leo 50
McLaglen, Victor 65, 75, 78, 80
Mac Laverty, Bernard 36

Index

Mac Liammóir, Micheál 13, 18, 26, 28, 66, 72, 94
Macnamara, Walter 43–44
Madison, Cleo 103
Maeve 34
Magee, Barney 44
Main, Marjorie 75
Major Barbara 60–61
Malden, A.B. 4
Mallin, Michael 45
Malo, Gina 17
Malone, Danny 27
Malone, Molly 73
Maloney, Grace 5
A Man Called Sloane 91
Man of Aran 48–49, 68
The Manions of America 92
Mankiowitz, Wolf 62
Manners, J. Hartley 107
Manning, Mary 19, 20, 68
Mannix, J. Edward 108
Mapes, Agnes 41
Marcus, Louis 33
Marion, Frank 40
Markey, Enid 73
The Marriage Circle 87
The Marriage of Molly-O 103
Marsh, Mae 73, 103
Marston, Theodore 53, 54
Martin, Herbert 24
Martin, Vivian 104
Mason, J.C. Bee 16
Mason, James 34
Mass Appeal 92
Masterpiece Theatre, Dublin 11, 14
Matchmaking in Ireland 9
Mathews, Kerwin 53
Matthews, Lester 22
Mature, Victor 61
Mayne, Herbert 9
Maytime in Mayfair 85
Meara, Anne 113
Meet the Quare Fellow 33
Meighan, Thomas 39–40, 73
Mein Leben für Irland 27
Melbourne-Cooper, Arthur 2–4
Meloney, William Brown 109
Men of Ireland 26–27
Menjou, Adolphe 73–74
Meredith, Burgess 71
Metropole Theatre, Dublin 17
Meyerhold, Vsevolod 55
Mia Films 94
Michael McShane, Matchmaker 43
Miles, Sarah 50
Miller, Charles 103
Miller, David 110
The Millionairess 62
Mills, John 50
Mills, Juliet 54
Mills, Michael 54
Minter, Mary Miles 84
The Miracle at Morgan's Creek 93
Mirren, Helen 36
Mirror of Ireland 28
Mise Éire 33
The Miser's Gift 14
Mitchell, Oswald 27
Mitchell, Thomas 54
Mitchum, Robert 34, 50
Mix, Tom 73
Moby Dick 51, 92
A Modern Salome 55
Moise, J. 10
Molly Entangled 104
The Molly Maguires 113
Mooney, Ria 22
Moore, Brian 63–64
Moore, Colleen 107
Moore, Edward 106
Moore, Emmett 22
Moore, Kieron 91
Moore, Matt 88
Moore, Owen 88
Moore, Thomas 107
Moore, Tom 88
Moran, Polly 107
Moran, Tom 10
Moreau, Jeanne 62
Morey, Harry 104
Morgan, Frank 76
Moriarty, D.A. 24
Morley, Robert 60, 62
Morrison, George 33
Morrow, Jeff 110
Moser, William 12
Mostel, Zero 62, 71
Mother Machree 75
Motion Picture Company of Ireland 35
Moulin Rouge 92
Mowbray, Alan 79
Mrs. Miniver 93
Mrs. O'Malley and Mr. Malone 75
Mrs. Warren's Profession 62

Mulhall, Jack 73
Mulkerns, Jim 49
Mullen, Pat 49
Mulligan, Richard 113
Mullins, Tommy 103
Murphy, Billy 24
Murphy, Edna 107
Murphy, Fidelma 112
Murphy, Joseph 42
Murphy, Miss K. 12
Murphy, Kathleen 13
Murphy, Pat 34–35
Murray, Charlie 102, 107, 109
Murray, Don 30
Murray, Mae 73
My Fair Lady 61, 63, 91
My Life for Ireland 27
My Wild Irish Rose 107

N

National Film Studios 31
National Films, Ltd. 15
National Portrait Gallery of Ireland 63
Nazimova, Alla 55, 85
Neilan, Marshall 107
Neill, Roy William 86
Neligan, Donal 51
Neptune's Daughter 15, 85
Never Put It in Writing 92, 112
New Brighton Tower Company 31
The New Gossoon 32
A New Gulliver 53
Newman, Paul 64
Newton, Robert 34, 60
Nicholls, George, Jr. 82
Nichols, Anne 101
Nichols, Dudley 80, 81, 82
NiGhrainne, Maire 112
The Night Fighters 91, 96
Night Life of the Gods 113
Noah's Ark 2
Nolan, Lloyd 75
Nolan, William Patrick 106
Nomads 92
Norah O'Neale 22
Normand, Mabel 73
Norris, Kathleen 108
Norris, Richard 101

O

Oberon, Merle 109
O'Brien, Edna 66
O'Brien, Niall 51, 113
O'Brien, Margaret 55
O'Brien, Pat 49, 75–76, 109
O'Cahill, Donal 24
O'Casey, Sean 81, 83, 94, 95
O'Connell, Marion 24
O'Connor, Frank 19, 66, 83, 109
O'Connor, Kate 4
O'Connor, Kathleen 12, 13
O'Connor, Pat 36
O'Connor, Una 82, 94, 98
Odd Man Out 34, 90, 97
O'Dea, Denis 82, 91, 111
O'Dea, Jimmy 10, 26, 83, 91
O'Donnell, Donovan 113
O'Donovan, Frank P. 103
O'Donovan, Fred 13
O'Donovan, Harry 26
O'Flaherty, Liam 66, 79
O Foghludha, Richard 9
O'Grady, Timothy E. 72
O'Hara, Barney 20
O'Hara, Charlie 103
O'Hara, Maureen 82, 89
O'Herlihy, Dan 90–91
O'Herlihy, Michael 112
Oidhche Sheanchais 49
Oisin 33
"The O'Kalems" 40–43
O'Keefe, Tom 103
Olcott, Sidney 40, 43
O'Leary, Colm 33
Olivier, Laurence 28, 62
Olsen, Moroni 82
O'Mahoney, Andy 72
O'Mahoney, Jerry 24
O'Malley, Kit 19
O'Malley, Pat 107
One of Ourselves 36
O'Neil, Sally 107
O'Neil of the Glens 12
O'Neill, Chris 72
O'Neill, Eugene 82
O'Neill, Máire 22, 95–96
O'Neill, Moire 112
The O'Neill 42, 43

Opera House, Cork 1
Ophuls, Marcel 34
O'Regan, Kathleen 27
Ormonde, Dr. 1
Ormsby-Scott, N. 15
O'Rorke, Peggy 19
Orphans of the Storm 87
O'Russ, Bob 68
O'Shea, Desmond 18
O'Shea, Milo 68, 91–92, 112
O'Sullivan, Brian 24, 26
O'Sullivan, Maureen 46, 89
O'Sullivan, Patrick 41
O'Toole, Peter 62, 91
Our Boys 38
Ourselves Alone 23
The Outsider 113–114

P

Paddy 92
Palace Cinema, Dublin 18
Palace Variety Theatre, Cork 1
Palmer, Lily 62
Parnell, Charles Stewart 110
Part Time Wife 108
Pascal, Gabriel 60–61
Passages from Finnegan's Wake 68
The Passing of the Third Floor Back 95
Patterson's Match Factory 9
Patton, Mrs. N.F. 13
Paul, Robert W. 1, 4
Paul, Vincent 1
Paxinou, Katina 63
Peacock Theatre, Dublin 20
Pearce, Michael 72
Pearls of the Crown 68
Pedelty, Donovan 21
Peg o' My Heart 94, 107
Peggy, the Will o' the Wisp 104
Pembroke, Scott 108
Peter Pan 85
Peters, House 86, 87
Petrova, Olga 104
Phillips, Bertram 16
Phillips, Leslie 32
Photo-Historic Company 5
Pickford, Mary 73, 88
The Picture of Dorian Gray 55
Picturesque Ireland 4
Pigs 38

Pike Theatre, Dublin 64
Plant, Jim 14
The Playboy of the Western World 23–24, 93
The Plough and the Stars 81–82, 96, 97, 98
Plunkett, James 91
The Poacher's Daughter 32
Poitin 38
Pollard, Harry 101
Pollock, George 32
Portrait of the Artist as a Young Man 70–71
Poteen 38
Potter, Maureen 70, 83
Powell, Frank 86, 87
Powell, Paul 103
Power, Tyrone 74, 83
Powers, William J. 18
Preminger, Otto 61, 62
Prendergast, Frank 37
Price, Dennis 23, 62
Price, Kate 102
Pride and Prejudice 93
Project One 64
Provincial Cinematograph Theatres 5, 68
PT-109 75
Ptushko, Alexander 53
Purcell, Noel 26, 30, 65, 83
Puttnam, David 36
Pygmalion 59–60

Q

The Quare Fellow 32–33
A Quiet Day in Belfast 37
The Quiet Man 82–83, 89, 96, 98
Quigley, Martin, Jr. 28
Quinn, Anthony 73
Quinn, Bob 38
Quinn, Patricia 113
Quish, D.P. 83

R

"Radharc" Film Unit 33
Radio Éireann 90
Radio Telefis Éireann 31, 33

Index

Rafferty at the Hotel De Rest 103
Rafferty Goes to Coney Island 103
Rafferty Settles the War 103
Rafferty's Rise 12
Ragtime 76
Rains, Claude 61
Rambova, Natacha 55
Random Harvest 93
Rascoe, Judith 70
Rathbone, Basil 54
Ray, Charles 73, 103
Raymond, Gary 23, 24
Rayner, Christine 53
The Razor's Edge 74
Rea, Stephen 35
Redgrave, Lynn 66
Redgrave, Michael 30, 56, 57
Redman, Joyce 89, 93
Reed, Carol 90
Reed, Donna 55
Reicher, Frank 104
Reid, Hal 106
Reilly, Jane 68
Reilly, Robert T. 112
Remington Steele 92
The Return of the Islander 49
Return to Glennascaul 28
Reynolds, T. O'Carroll 9
Reynolds, Vera 108
Rich, Irene 55
Richardson, Sir Ralph 54, 113
Richman, Harry 89
Riders to the Sea 22-23
Riley the Cop 79
The Rising of the Moon 26, 74, 79, 83, 96
Ritt, Martin 113
The Rivals 54
Roaming the Emerald Isle with Will Rogers 46
Roberts, Valentine 13
Robertson, Cliff 75
Robinson, Edward G. 54
Robison, Arthur 79
Robson, Flora 61, 83
Rock, William "Pop" 104
Rock of Ages 16
The Rocking Horse Winner 93
Rocky Road to Dublin 33-34
Roeves, Maurice 69, 112
Rogers, Charles 101
Rogers, Sean 22

Roland, Ruth 73
Roman Boxera 57
The Romance of Elaine 86
A Romance of Puck Fair 12
Rome, Stewart 17
Romeo and Juliet 92
Rory O'More 42
Rosaleen Dhu 18
Rose Marie 87
Rose of Tralee 27
Rosenthal, Joe 18
Rosmer, Milton 17, 55
Rotunda, Dublin 1, 5, 14, 43, 44-45
Rudden, Rev. Thomas F. 107
The Ruling Class 91
Rush, Barbara 110
Rutherford, Margaret 56, 57
Ruttman, Walter 68
Ryan, Kathleen 34, 110
Ryan, Mae 22
Ryan's Daughter 49-51

S

Sackville Street Picture House 4-5, 13
Saint Joan 57, 61-62
St. John Barry, Tom 66
St. Leger, Bill 72
Sally's Irish Rogue 32
Salome 55
Sanders, George 55
Saoirse? 33
Sargent, Fay 10
Saturday Night and Sunday Morning 93
Savage, Henry 23
Scenes of Irish Life in Dublin 43
Schauffler, Elsie T. 110
Schneider, Edwin 46
The School for Scandal 54
Schuster, Harold 47
Scott, Michael 83
The Search for Bridey Murphy 111
Seberg, Jean 61
Second Honeymoon 74
Selig Polyscope Company 99
Sellers, Peter 62
Sennett, Mack 73
A Sense of Loss 34

Seven Footprints to Satan 87
7th Heaven 92
Sextant Films 83
Seyler, Athene 22
Shake Hands with the Devil 30, 91
The Shamrock and the Rose 102
The Shamrock Handicap 78
Shamus O'Brien 102, 103
Shannon, Peggy 103
The Shaughraun 107
Shaun Rhue 42
Shaw, George Bernard 57–63
Shaw, Harold 17
Shaw, Robert 63
She Stoops to Conquer 53, 54
She Wore a Yellow Ribbon 75, 98
Sheen, Martin 64
Sheldon, Roy 106
Sheridan, Dinah 21
Sheridan, John D. 66
Sheridan, Richard Brinsley 54, 63
Shields, Arthur 12, 13, 82, 94, 98
Shields, Brooke 65
Shiels, George 32
Shiels, Una 19
Shostak, Murray 54
Side Street 88
Sidney, George 101, 102, 109
Silvester, Chris 10
Sim, Alastair 62
Simmons, Jean 61, 63, 65
Sims, Sylvia 32
Sinbad the Sailor 89
Sinclair, Arthur 22
Sinful Davy 51
Sing as We Go 95
The Singing Fool 19
Sipra, Mahmoud 31
Sirk, Douglas 110
Sixty Glorious Years 85
Smiling Irish Eyes 107
Smith, Albert E. 104
Smith, Sir C. Aubrey 56
Smith, Maggie 83
Smith, Thorne 113
The Smuggler's Lass 103
A Son of Erin 103
Song o' My Heart 46–47, 89, 108
The Spanish Main 89
Spring in Park Lane 85
Stafford, Brendan 33
Stahl, John 110

Staircase 91
Stanmore, Frank 54
Stanton, Pat 27
Stanwyck, Barbara 54, 82
Star of Erin Music Hall, Dublin 1
Stark, Pauline 103
Steele, Tommy 113
Steiner, Max 80
Stephenson, Henry 109
Stevens, Roy 50
Stewart, Douglas Day 65
Stoker, Abraham 63
Stone, Andrew S. 111
Stoney, George 48
Storm in a Teacup 95
Stradling, Harry 55
The Stranger's Banquet 65
Strick, Joseph 68, 69, 70, 71
Strode, Woody 61
Strumpet City 91
Stuart, Binkie 27
Stuart, Madge 17, 54
The Stuntman 91
Sturges, Preston 62
Sullivan, Francis L. 61
Sullivan, James Mark 11
Sullivan, Joe 103
Sunderland, Scott 60
The Supreme Passion 107
Sutherland, A. Edward 101
Swain, Mack 102
Sweet Inniscara 22
Sweet Rosie O'Grady 107
Swift, Jonathan 53
Synge, John Millington 22, 23

T

Tale of a Million 92
Taliaferro, Mabel 104
Tank Training School in Ireland 5
"Tarzan" series 89
Taylor, Laurette 107
Taylor, Rod 83
Taylor, William Desmond 84
Ten Days Leave 9
Tennyson, Walter 54
A Terrible Beauty 34, 91, 96
Terry, Alice 103

Terry, Ellen 104
Terry-Lewis, Mabel 56
Thanhouser Company 53
This Land Is Mine 89
This Other Eden 32
This Sporting Life 91, 93
Thomas, Olive 73
Thomas, Queenie 16, 54
Thornby, Robert 104
Thorndike, Russell 54
Thorndike, Sybil 30, 57, 60
The Three Worlds of Gulliver 53
Thunderball 92
Tobin, Niall 51
Todd, Richard 55, 61
Tom Sawyer 84
Top o' the Morning 96, 110
The Top o' the Morning 107
Torchy Plays with Dynamite 87
Torn Curtain 64
Tracy, Spencer 75, 76, 82
The Travels of Jaimie McPheeters 91
Travers, Ben 63
Tree, David 60
A Tree Grows in Brooklyn 75
The Trial of Mary Dugan 2
Trilby 87
Trimble, Larry 43
Trodd, Kenith 37
Tryon, Tom 113
Tully, Montgomery 89
Tushingham, Rita 66
Tutin, Dorothy 56
Two Blocks Away 101
The Two Orphans 85
Tyrone, Kathleen 27

U

Ulster Group Theatre, Belfast 93
Ulster Literary Theatre, Belfast 93
Ulysses 68-70, 91
Ulysses in Nighttown 71
An Unfunny Love Affair 12
Ure, Mary 63

V

Valentino, Rudolph 39, 85
Van Druten, John 110
Van Eyck, Peter 32
Van Heusen, James 110
Vanna, Nina 54
Vekroff, Perry 104
Los Viajes de Gulliver 53
The Vicar of Wakefield 53
Victim of His Imagination 63
Victor, Henry 17, 55
Victoria the Great 85
Vignola, Robert 40, 41
Vitagraph Company 43, 104-106
The Vixen 113
The Voice of Ireland 20-21
Volta Theatre 66-68
Von Rathony, Akos 62
Vousden, Valentine 19

W

W.B. Yeats: A Tribute 66
Wakely, Phyllis 18
Walbrook, Anton 61
Wald, Jerry 69
Waller, Leslie 113
Walsh, J. Theobold 5, 6, 8
Walsh, Kay 21
Walsh, William J. 9
War Brides 85
Warde, Ernest 53, 104
Warner, David 38
Warren, "Cyclone" Billy 9
Watts, Tom 16
Way Down East 87
Wee Willie Winkie 75
Weigle, Captain Edwin F. 46
Welles, Orson 28, 90
Wesson, Craig 113
Westcott, Netta 55
When Knights Were Bold 98
When Love Comes to Gavin 14
White, Chrissie 53
White, Pearl 86, 87
The White House 91

Whitten, Norman 8–11
Whitten, Vernon 9
Whom the Gods Destroy 104–106
Wicklow Gold 10
Widmark, Richard 61
Widow Malone 12
Wiene, Robert 55
Wilbur, Crane 73
Wilcox, Herbert 85–86
Wilde, Oscar 54–57
Wilding, Michael 56
Williams, Emlyn 60
Williams, Eric 54
Willy Reilly and His Colleen Bawn 14
Wilson, Lois 39
Wings of the Morning 47–48, 65
With Will Rogers in Dublin 46
The Woman God Changed 65
A Woman of No Importance 55
Woman's Wit 14
Woods, Arthur 22
Works, J.G. 113
Wright, Teresa 111
Wynter, Dana 30
Wynyard, Diana 56

Y

A Yank at Oxford 89
Yanova, Varvara 55
The Years Between 26
Yeats, William Butler 15, 66, 72, 94
Yeats Country 33, 66
You Can't Beat the Irish 92
Young, Alan 61
Young, Robert 55
Young, Tammany 103
Young Cassidy 83–84
Ypres 14

Z

Zardoz 49